MW01609917

POVERTY, CHASTITY AND DISOBEDIENCE:
My Six Years in a Catholic Convent

SUSAN MATTERN

"Coming from her parent's small house directly from high school, the convent motherhouse seemed like a medieval castle, minus the Prince Charming, of course."

Susan Mattern had no problem with most of the vows when she entered the convent. Poverty was easy. She didn't have any possessions, joining the convent directly from high school. Chastity was no big deal, since she hadn't ever met a boy she liked. But obedience? That was a problem, especially when the rules made no sense.

Sometimes humorous, often serious, this memoir tells of Susan Mattern's attempt to become a nineteenth century nun in a twentieth century world while the rest of her age group experimented with drugs and sex.

Poverty, Chastity and Disobedience
Chapter 1

March, 1966

I grabbed the mail, opened the front door of my house, and even though it was too early for them to be home, called out "Mom, Dad?" I stopped rehearsing my speech to them as I spotted a large white envelope addressed to "Miss Susan Mattern," with a Washington University logo.

Walking into my bedroom, I dropped my textbooks on the bed, tore open the envelope and read the letter quickly. My heart skipped a beat. A full four-year scholarship to Washington University in St. Louis, my hometown. My parents would be so proud. I was the first daughter of three to go to college, and now I had a much-needed and prestigious scholarship. But the tight lump in my throat choked any thrill I might have had. A year ago, this would have been a dream come true. Now it was just another hurdle to jump over, and it couldn't have come at a worse time. I had to tell my parents tonight.

My school uniform--plaid skirt, white blouse and blazer-- got thrown on my unmade bed as I searched in the closet for jeans and a flowery blouse. It felt good to take off the uniform, even though it crossed my mind that I'd be wearing a uniform forever.

I heard the front door close. "Sue, are you home?" my mom called out.

"Yes." I walked out to the kitchen after I changed, bringing most of the mail. Mom was already sitting at the grey formica table, a few textbooks around her, with a fresh piece of paper ready. She asked me about my day just as I asked her the same question. We laughed and decided both our days had been pretty good. She had come from class, still neatly dressed in her blue suit, with her grey hair in the current bouffant style, and her pearl earrings in place.

She was getting her Missouri teaching credential at the

same time I was going to high school. Even at age fifty-seven, she was excited about learning new things.

We'd sit at the kitchen table in the evenings, both studying. She'd been a teacher in my old Catholic school but wanted to get her teaching credential so she could teach in the public schools for more money.

I set the table while Mom heated up the dinner, all the while wondering if I should tell them about the scholarship first or second, after my other big news. Dad had gotten home and I called him from his basement woodworking shop. Dinner was left-over spaghetti from Rugerrios Italian restaurant and politics served up as usual. All we ever talked about at dinner was politics. The Arch was finally finished, about to be dedicated, and the vice-president was coming to town for the ceremony. I was happy listening to them talk--and putting off what I was going to say for as long as possible. We ate in between talking. At last mom pushed back her chair and I said, "Wait."

Pulling out the folded letter from the pocket of my jeans, I handed it first to mom.

She read it, smiling, and I saw tears in her eyes. She handed it to dad. Oh, this was going to be so much harder than I had ever dreamed. I realized then I should have told them my other news first and waited to tell them about the scholarship later. Well, it was too late for that now.

"We're so proud of you," Mom said as she handed the letter to Dad. He smiled and laughed happily. "That's vonderful. Ve knew you could do it!" His German accent was still strong even after forty years.

The moment had come. I swallowed hard, "I need to tell you something."

"Oh," Mom said, a little puzzled, but probably wondering which university I'd finally chosen. I'd received partial scholarships to St. Louis University and been accepted at Oberlin and Wellesley.

I blurted the words out, my careful speech forgotten. "I'm not going to go to Washington or St. Louis University in the fall. I've decided to enter the convent."

"What?" Mom's smile disappeared immediately. "The

4

convent?"

My dad looked at Mom and said, "Vhat? Vhat does she mean?"

"She wants to become a nun, like the nuns who teach her at school!"

He said with a frown, "I don't understand. Vhat does that mean?"

This was my only chance to convince them. I looked directly at Mom. She knew the church. Dad didn't. He had become Catholic to marry my mom over thirty years ago and had never set foot in a church again. She could explain it to him later.

But before I could say a word, Mom looked at me with disbelief and said, "You never wanted to be a nun! You've told me that hundreds of times. Remember that essay you wrote in 8th grade about how you didn't have a vocation. You won first prize!"

"I remember," I said lamely, the embarrassment still fresh in my mind, "but I really want to become a teacher like you and help people."

"You don't have to be a nun to do that!"

"I know, but the convent has changed. It's way more modern and it's only going to get better since the Vatican Council. I want to be part of that new liberal church."

Mom shook her head sadly. "From what you've told me about the nuns at your school, they haven't changed at all."

She was right. All I had done the last four years was complain about the nuns and their archaic ways of doing things. And she had taught in a Catholic school, knew the nuns, and didn't think much of them.

"It takes time," I tried to explain. "All the young people going in like me are the ones who are going to change it."

"What about your education? You've worked so hard." She wiped away a tear.

I felt better answering that question.

"They have their best teachers at the motherhouse, because they're in charge of teaching all the teachers and preparing them. I'll get a really good education. They have a four-year college and I can major in English and music--and get my teaching credential." That wasn't exactly what I wanted to say. My carefully prepared speech sounded a lot better when I had said it to myself without any interruptions. I knew I wasn't doing a very good job.

My dad sat quietly, listening but not understanding. We weren't what you would call a "religious" family. A lot of Catholic families in the sixties prided themselves on being Catholic, hoping that at least one child would enter the seminary or the convent. Those families would go to Mass every Sunday since it was a mortal sin not to go, but they would also go to Mass during the week for extra points. They'd always sit in the front pews, volunteering for all the parish events, and being a large part of the Catholic community.

My family wasn't like that. Mom believed in God and to a lesser degree, the church, but didn't care much for the nuns and priests she taught with at my old elementary school. She felt most of them were hypocrites, acting holy and pious, but being mean and petty in real life. My mom felt that the priests gave useless advice about marriage and children, subjects they knew nothing about, and received their monthly salary without much real work.

My two older sisters didn't care anything about religion or church. By the time I got to high school, they had both gone to secretarial school, dated a lot, and had gotten married.

I had gone to a Catholic school for all twelve of my school years. Learning about God--or more importantly--how to be a good Catholic--was an everyday lesson. Most of my classmates didn't seem to care much about God or religion, but I took it very seriously. I really did believe that God was the reason for our whole life. He had created me for a reason--he had created the whole universe, and it made sense for me to discover why He had made me.

A nun named Sister Angeline taught my first grade class. She frightened me. She stood in front of the classroom and even though I sat in the back row, I shriveled down in my desk for most of the day, hoping her anger and ruler wouldn't find me. I'm sure I never said a word that entire year.

She was tiny but clothed completely in black and had small snake-like eyes that would fix on one of us, then another in rapid succession. She had complete control over the sixty students in her classroom, and there was never any talking or misbehaving.

6

She held a blue book in her hand, the same Baltimore catechism that each one of us had on our desks but could barely read. She asked the daily questions, "Why did God make you?" and we answered by rote, "God made me to know Him, to love Him, to serve Him in this world, and to be happy with Him forever in the next."

Sister Angeline taught us lots of theology, sprinkled with her personal opinions. She said eternity with God was going to be wonderful, like eating ice cream every day. The ice cream sounded okay to me as a first grader, but even then, the idea of having it every day for all eternity didn't sound like much fun.

I never once doubted the existence of God. As I got older, I often wondered about the church and its rules. A lot of them didn't make any sense, and by the time I reached high school I knew God was much bigger than any church.

After all, He had created the universe and everything in it. He was love and compassion and acceptance, although I did wonder how He could allow so much evil in the world. The search for the real God was very important to me and I really believed that I should and would spend my life serving Him. Only I wasn't sure how to go about doing that.

I tried to see beyond the institution and see the God behind it all. I truly believed and never doubted for a moment the reality of what I had learned in my Baltimore Catechism so many years before. I had grown up, but the words were still true. We were created to know God, to love Him and to serve Him. I never once questioned those basics, but looking at my mom's tears, I knew this would be a hard sell.

Mom kept shaking her head in disbelief. "But don't you want to get married and have a family?"

"No, not really." I felt bad saying it, but it was the truth.

My sisters, nine and eleven years older than me, were both married. I wasn't impressed with either one of their husbands. Jane's husband was rich, but he seemed overly proud of himself and his status. He had picked Jane up for their first date in his aunt's Rolls Royce. And since no one in my family knew anyone who owned a Rolls Royce, it was a big selling point.

Carol's husband didn't seem very intelligent and I had no

idea what she saw in him. I was in my "Bach and Shakespeare" phase and he wasn't interested at all in any kind of culture. He liked beer and football and I dismissed him completely. My sisters both had young children. I babysat my nieces once and that was enough. Crying and diapers and feeding and no, that wasn't for me. Marriage and a family didn't sound like anything I was going to miss.

I kept talking, trying to convince both of my parents.

"I want to dedicate my life to God, find out more about Him, and help people. It's kind of like the Peace Corps, only with religion."

I was proud of my comparison. The Vatican Council in 1962 had upended the whole church, changing Latin to English, and giving a larger role to women, almost equal to men. And in a few more years, women would have the ability to become priests and be on an equal footing with men. It would happen soon.

"Is this because of that nun you're friends with?" Mom frowned.

She was talking about Sister Rachel, who taught English and speech at my high school. We had become good friends during my senior year.

"No, it's my own decision. She's never said a word to me about joining."

I couldn't tell them how much my decision did have to do with S. Rachel. She was a huge influence--and most of the reason I had changed my mind about nuns. She showed me that the church, with its many flaws, was becoming more modern, more liberal, and might be a good place to continue my search. She was young, intelligent, did what she wanted, thought what she wanted. She was free to be her own person. She loved teaching, and we spent hours talking about English and religion and philosophy. She was a symbol of the person I wanted to be. And I realized I could pursue all my interests, English, music, learning about God, in the convent.

My father was quiet during the whole conversation. Not only did he know nothing about the church, but he also didn't pay much attention to his children's lives. He worked hard at his job and on weekends he played tennis. In the evenings he watched TV.

8

My dad and I had never had a heart-to-heart talk about anything.

They were both sitting quietly. My mom kept wiping tears off her cheek. I kept talking to fill up the space, and I knew I wasn't doing a very good job of it. It was the first time I had really tried to explain my decision to anyone.

"I'll be able to major in English and music, and I'll be getting a degree--and a teaching credential. It's a really good college. They have their best teachers there," I repeated, not knowing what else to say. "This is really what I want to do."

"It's just so unnatural, though," my mom persisted. "I hate to see you missing out on marriage and a family."

I bristled at that remark. "I don't think it's unnatural. I mean, the church really respects nuns and priests and encourages people to have vocations."

I knew as I said it that the argument wouldn't convince mom. Mom knew how much I loved my summer school classes in a public school where I was finally treated as an intelligent student. I had teachers at summer school who told me I should go to Radcliffe or Wellesley. They knew I was smart. The nuns at my high school never noticed, even when I became a National Merit Finalist. But when I met Sister Rachel, she was the first nun who really appreciated me.

Until about six months ago I had completely agreed with my mom. But I realized now, with young people like me and Sister Rachel, the church was getting more liberal every day.

My dad ended the conversation, "Vell, I just vant you to be happy. That's all."

"I think I will be," I said simply.

Mom didn't say anything else, but her silence said everything.

The conversation was over. It had gone the best it could have, I guessed. I hoped that we would talk more about it, but I wasn't going to change my mind. I was eighteen years old, and I was certain I knew what I was doing. My mom got up, followed by my dad, and they walked the few feet into their bedroom.

Our house that my father had built was only 700 sq. feet, and as I washed the dishes I could hear them talking. There were four small rooms connected by the square hall in the middle, so it was impossible not to hear snatches of conversation.

"But the scholarship…Washington University….her music….that nun….just don't understand….happy….she's young….can leave….change her mind."

I walked into my room and closed the door. I felt bad about my mom. I really respected her opinion but she didn't even listen to mine anymore. Part of that was my fault. Our family didn't "do" feelings very well. I remember how often Mom would say, "You don't really feel that way." And I never argued with her. I just figured that even if I did feel a certain way, it wasn't anything to be shared. Our whole family got along very well. The surface was calm—no arguments or waves allowed, but I often wondered what was beneath the surface. Talking about politics and current events was a convenient way to not talk about anything else, even though I was only dimly aware of that family dynamic at the time.

So this news had come as a surprise to them both, because it had never been discussed or even mentioned. But Mom probably would've still hated my decision even if we had talked or argued about it for months.

My dad wasn't nearly as upset as my mom. He had his work and his tennis, and if his children were happy, he was happy.

There was more to my decision than just the church reforms. I had a fascination with religion all my life. I wanted to know more about God and why people believed. The institution of the church wasn't the best place to find God, but I also knew there were amazing, forward thinking, liberal women who would be teaching me. I wanted to find people who shared my fascination with God.

I couldn't really put that into words for my parents. But I hoped I had explained enough for them to be satisfied. I looked in the mirror over my dresser, wondering what I would look like in the habit. I knew I wasn't very pretty--going to an all-girls high school hadn't helped in the dating department--but even in co-ed summer school no boy had ever glanced in my direction. I knew the habit was ugly, but I didn't really care. It wouldn't make any difference anyway.

My hair, styled in the bouffant style that everyone wore,

looked puffy and fake and a boring brown, but that would all be covered up. My face was a little too long, and my nose was way too large for my face, a trait I had inherited from my German father. It looked okay on him but was way too big for me. I caught myself worrying about my features and realized that I shouldn't be worrying about things like that. I had more important things to think about, like spiritual things, and studying.

It was raining hard the next morning as I ran the long block to the bus stop. By the time I got on, my bouffant hair had flattened and I sat in the empty backseat, trying not to be overwhelmed by the overpowering smell of stale bus, old perfume and wet bodies. My good friend Pam got on in Wellston, the black area of town, just fifteen minutes south of where I lived in Jennings. My neighborhood was a complete contrast to Pam's--it was completely white. Nobody in my family cared, but if a black family had moved in, I was pretty sure half the people would be selling their homes within a week. I waved to her and she sat down next to me, trying to close her umbrella and balance her books at the same time. Her hair, carefully ironed, was already frizzy.

Pam was one of the six girls entering the convent from our senior class, and the one I was closest to. She shook her head, droplets scattering everywhere. The bus lurched forward. We had almost an hour ride to our high school in the city.

"Did you tell them?" she looked at me, her brown eyes wide with worry.

"Yeah," I answered hesitantly.

"Well? What did they say?"

"They weren't happy, that's for sure. Oh, and I got a four-year scholarship to Washington University in the mail yesterday."

"Oh, Susie, that's wonderful." Pam's face lit up as she grabbed my arm in excitement. Then the smile slid off her face.

"Oh, no. What did you do?"

"I shouldn't have showed them the letter from Washington University first."

"Well, you kind of had to, didn't you? They had to know sometime."

"Yeah, but it sure didn't help the conversation."

I looked at Pam. "When are you going to tell your

parents?"

"Tonight, for sure."

"Do you think they'll be okay with it?"

She smiled her big smile. "They'll be fine with it, especially my daddy. One of their daughters—a nun! They'll be so proud, Susie." She looked down at her books, a little embarrassed.

"Hey, that's okay. I'm glad somebody will be happy about going into the convent. And my parents will get better."

"Oh, Susie, I know they will! I just know it." Pam was always optimistic. She loved my parents from the few times she had met them, especially my dad. She laughed at his jokes and he loved her and her stories.

I stared out the window. I knew my mom never would get any better, but I didn't know what to do about it.

We transferred busses and talked about our English test that day. We were quiet for a while as we passed the mansions overlooking Forest Park and went by the Chase Park Plaza, the swankiest hotel in St. Louis. Our high school was coming up soon.

Pam grabbed my arm. "Susie, do you think we're doing the right thing? I mean, are we crazy, joining the convent?"

I looked down at my books. "Everybody else thinks we are, that's for sure. I haven't met one person who thinks it's a good idea. I just don't know anymore."

The bus rolled past the massive St. Louis Cathedral and stopped. We got up, walked quickly down the aisle, stepped off and ran quickly inside our high school.

"See you later," she called.

I stood dripping in the hall, rearranging my books at my locker for my morning classes. I'd given up on my hair, and the homeroom bell was about to ring. Pam's question hung in the air around me. Were we crazy? I didn't know.

I couldn't explain my decision to my parents very well because for all my arguments, I didn't really know why I was joining the convent. I was very liberal and believed in equal rights for women. I knew the convent was conservative. But I was joining the convent not of the present, but of the future, made up of highly educated women who could change the world. I wanted to be part of that group. I had moments when I wondered if S. Rachel

12

was unusual, that maybe she didn't really represent the future, but I put that thought away quickly and ran to class.

Chapter 2
The Shoes

At the end of May I graduated from high school. I was thrilled to be finished and on to the next part of my life. I attended my last creative writing class at Mark Twain Summer Institute where I became the editor of the literary magazine. It was a special summer school for gifted students from all over the St. Louis area, and I had been attending every summer for four years. I wanted to work one last time with Mr. Read, my favorite teacher. I'd had a crush on him for the last four years. A Bostonian with a Kennedy-like accent, he dressed in tweed jackets with outrageous striped and polka-dot ties, and had a summer home in Taxco, Mexico. He exuded coolness, and he hinted that the books he wrote were banned somewhere back East. I tried to find them, but since he informed us he wrote under a pen name, I never could. He was in his forties, and although I dreamed of a wild romance with him, consisting of a kiss or two, I knew it was just an infatuation.

I went to lunch every day with my friend Carol from summer school. I wanted to have as much fun as possible in my last few months of freedom.

I told Mr. Read on the last day of class that I was joining the convent in the fall. He gave me a strange look and said, "Why in God's name are you doing that? I thought you'd go to Radcliffe or Wellesley or at least Washington University."

I replied with my now familiar refrain of being a teacher and helping people.

"Why do you have to be a nun to do that?'

"So I can dedicate my life to God and help people that way."

"You will be going to college, won't you?"

"Yes, I'll get my degree in English and music--and my teaching credential."

"Well, good luck," he said without any enthusiasm. "You know, you have a lot of talent and you did a great job this summer. I hope you're happy with your new life. And don't waste all that

14

talent."

He shook my hand and that was it. I left on the bus to go home and he probably left for his summer home in Mexico. No one seemed to be happy about my decision except for our small group of convent-bound friends.

Even though I was used to taking the bus everywhere, my mother insisted that I learn how to drive.

"But I won't be driving a car any time soon." I complained.

"I know, but after you graduate, what if you are stationed in some town outside the state? I want you to be able to get home--for visits," she added quickly. She was adamant that I learn to drive.

I reluctantly agreed. I had to agree to some suggestions of hers since I knew she was so unhappy about my convent decision. Mom took me out in our old white Plymouth Valiant, a stick shift, and I practiced in parking lots, then streets with hills, then the highway, until I got my license.

One day I received a letter from the convent listing all the clothes I'd need. I walked into the living room that evening. Mom was reading a book while dad was watching the Cardinals on TV.

I handed her the letter. "Mom, I need to get a few clothes for next year. Would you mind helping me get them? I'm sure they won't cost very much." After all, I was only paying a hundred dollars for my entire college education, which was an incredible bargain. I was giving my whole life to them, but at the time, it seemed like a good deal.

"They'll provide the habit, but I have to get t-shirts, bras, a couple of white nightgowns and shoes."

"Sure," Mom tried to look pleased, like it was a fun mother-daughter shopping trip, but her mouth couldn't quite manage a smile.

"I have to get the shoes down on Grand Avenue, that's the only place in the city that sells them."

"Ok, we can go this Saturday, if you want."

I wondered what the shoes would look like, but I'd seen what all the other nuns wore and I wasn't very hopeful that these would be any different.

The first week of August my mom and I drove downtown to buy my shoes. The shoe store was on Grand Avenue, which might have been grand eighty years ago, but by 1966 was just old. The faded red brick building had a real store on the ground floor with display windows. The shoe store was stuck on the fourth floor.

We walked into the ancient elevator and waited as the elevator operator announced the floors. He was young, looked bored, his trousers seemed dusty, and his small red hat was off to the side with a string under his chin. He said, "Fourth floor" in a monotone. We stepped out into the musty hall, and the carpet stretched its thin threads desperately across the hall. The long corridor was filled with doors leading to offices. A few out-of-place picture windows faced the hall and were filled with clothes. The shoe store had a dusty window with two mannequins dressed in gray dresses with white sandals on their old smooth feet. They stared vacantly out the window to the wall beyond.

As we opened the door, a little brass bell tinkled. A few chairs lined the walls like a doctor's office and the faded reddish-brown carpet intruded from the hallway. A small white-haired man came out from behind a dark curtain with a look of surprise and asked softly, "Can I help you?"

I showed him the list and he knew exactly what I wanted. Well, it wasn't what I wanted. It's what I had to get.

Mom and I sat down carefully in the split red vinyl chairs while he measured my feet. "Size 10," he proclaimed, trying to add some excitement. My mom had told me years ago that Jackie Kennedy wore the same shoe size as I did, but unfortunately that was the only thing I had in common with the former First Lady. I didn't have her looks, her money, her name or her social status. All I shared was her shoe size, so even though my mother meant well, the comparison didn't make me feel any better about my feet--or my life.

A shoe that looks nice in a size five looks completely different in a size ten. It isn't just bigger. It's hard to explain, but it looks much uglier than anything in a size five. Even though I knew that, I wasn't prepared to see the black boat-like shoes that frankly looked terrible even in a size five. In my size they seemed to take over the whole room, like some ocean liner gliding into port.

My decision to join the convent was based on theology,

philosophy, and a real desire to find God. Looking at the shoes brought me down to earth quickly. I was so sure and proud of my choice, but suddenly, looking at the hideous shoes, I wondered if I was making the right decision.

Why did I have to wear these "boats" just because I wanted to serve God? It made no sense. The salesman put them on my feet and laced them up. I stood and walked a few steps to a full-length mirror. They were even more awful, doubled in the mirror and quadrupled in the reflections beyond. I could tell my mother was embarrassed for me, because she sat very still and quiet. What could she say? "Oh, Sue, those look lovely? You look like an old lady." I guess it was better that she sat quietly. I was completely embarrassed on my own. I didn't want to look at the shoes for more than a second in the full-length mirror.

The salesman admonished me to walk around in them for a while, to make sure they were comfortable. I quickly assured him they were. They felt okay for two minutes. I had no idea how they'd feel after twelve or fourteen hours.

He and my mom chatted about all sorts of things. As I had my back to them and was looking in the mirror, I heard him whisper, "Don't worry, a lot of them leave." I sat down, and he took them off my embarrassed feet. I needed two pairs of them. I hadn't heard my mom's answer, but I remember thinking that what he said was rude. I don't remember much else except the incredible width and length and breadth of the shoes. The embarrassment wasn't over. I had to see the gigantic boxes they came in and we had to carry them out of the building, like luggage for a long overseas trip. At least no one knew what was in them. We got home, and I put the boxes far back in my closet and tried to forget that I'd be wearing them in about a month. I was still sure, (well, mostly sure), that I had made the right decision.

Chapter 3
Entrance Day

August, 1966

I took a last look at my tiny bedroom where I had lived for the first eighteen years of my life. I wasn't sure when I would see it again.

The blinds were down to shade the room from the August heat. My old green patchwork quilt covered my twin bed. The pull-down maple desk stood silently in the corner. It had little doors and cubbyholes that had been hiding places for dolls and toys when I was younger. My closet was filled with brightly colored clothes. I wasn't taking any of them. The clothes provided in the convent were called habits; they were all black.

I felt bad about leaving my house and my life, but I felt the worst about leaving my large radio, the size of a microwave, the source of so much beautiful music for many years. I was a classical pianist. I loved Bach, Beethoven and Chopin. Every night I listened to my favorite classical music station, after I had practiced on our little Baldwin spinet in the living room. I hoped I'd have a chance to listen to music in the motherhouse.

Mom came up behind me. "Are you ready?" She was trying to sound happy but couldn't quite hide the sadness in her voice. I was quite glad that our family didn't do "feelings" well, because I wasn't at all sure how I was feeling, especially today.

"I guess so." I wanted to sound excited but had a catch in my throat. It was hard to walk away from all I had ever known. I really wanted to enter the convent, but as the day got closer, my excitement had worn off, replaced by anxiety.

And now the day was here. Even though it was Sunday, we hadn't gone to church. We had to be at the motherhouse at two o'clock.

The stagnant air was wet and sticky in the August heat. It oozed inside our small house, and our one tiny window air conditioner in the living room couldn't keep it away. The fans just blew the hot air from room to room.

My dad, laughing and joking as usual, pulled my new black

trunk out of my room and into the cooler living room.

"Vhat do you have in here?" he groaned, as he pretended it was heavier than it really was. I ran over to help him with it, but he brushed me away.

"I can get it for you," he smiled. It was filled with convent regulation t-shirts, bras, black stockings, and underwear. A few favorite piano and English books were thrown on top, since I was going to major in music and English at the college.

I walked into the kitchen to grab a final coke. I didn't know of any "coke" regulations, but I couldn't imagine the convent ordering cases of soft drinks when water would work just as well.

As I sipped its syrupy sweetness, I took a last look at our back yard. Outside our kitchen window was the huge plum tree with its spreading branches that shadowed half the yard. The bluish-purple fruit hung like garnets among the green leaves. Those hours I had sat on my favorite branch, dreaming of my future life, seemed so long ago. Further out in the yard I could see the swing set that dad had built for me, bigger than any playground swing. I had been so proud of it. My friends and I used to swing back and forth as high as we could pump our little legs. The splintery wooden seats with their peeling red paint were up and hooked around the metal bars, no longer in use.

I had spoken to my sister Jane in New York a few days earlier, and I already said goodbye to Carol, who lived in north St. Louis. They were nine and eleven years older than I, and I didn't really know them very well. They thought I was out of my mind to enter the convent but were too busy with their own lives to say much.

I hadn't gotten any congratulations on my decision to enter religious life except from a few nuns. The usual reaction from everyone else was, "Why on earth are you becoming a nun?"

I was getting tired of explaining it when I couldn't really explain it to myself. I just knew it was the right decision for me. It bothered me that I couldn't put it into words.

I finished my coke, looked sadly around the kitchen for one last time and walked in the living room. Dad and I pulled the trunk to the front door, carried it down the porch steps, and out to our old car.

As we loaded the trunk in the car, Dolores, our sweet next-door neighbor, came running out to say goodbye to me.

"Oh, good luck!" she said, out of breath. "I just know you'll be happy." She was a model Catholic, and probably wished at least one of her boys would become a priest, but neither had shown any inclination to do that.

Old Mrs. Ruthmeyer even walked across the street to say a few words. She knew everybody's business because she sat at her front window and watched whatever was going on up and down the block. One time an Indian gentleman had come to pick up my dad for a game of tennis. They hadn't been gone a minute before our telephone rang and she asked my mom bluntly, "Was that man a Negro?"

"No, he's from India."

"Oh, that's ok," Mrs. Ruthmeyer said sweetly. "I thought he might have been a Negro."

My parents couldn't stand racists. I couldn't either. Our neighborhood was still white, but we were all waiting for the day when a black family bought a house. Everyone would sell their homes as quickly as possible and get out. My parents had already decided they didn't care who lived next to them. Anyway, watching Mrs. Ruthmeyer actually come out of her door meant that my joining the convent was a pretty important event.

I said my quick goodbyes and we got in the car. The ride from north to south St. Louis took about a half hour. None of us said much. Not much had been said since March, when I told them about my decision.

"Give her a few months," some friends had said to her, "She'll be out soon." I knew she thought I would come to my senses. I was a polite and shy person and never spoke up, but whenever I heard people say that I felt so angry, and it made me even more determined to prove them wrong.

We took highway 70 past the old small arms plant, built during the Second World War, down past the brand new Arch, gleaming silver in the sunlight, the Anheuser-Busch brewery which always smelled like cherry pie to me, and then got off the highway and went south along the Mississippi River till we were way past the city. The directions said to turn left on Ripa Avenue,

20

and we drove by some tiny brick houses, a large high school, and then the road ended in the parking lot next to the looming red brick motherhouse.

Two young smiling sisters came out of the building, helped us with the trunk, and then disappeared with it. Another tall thin sister, Sister Philippa, told us that it had been taken to the trunk room in the basement.

"And who are you?" she asked, looking very businesslike.

"Susan Mattern," I answered as she looked through a packet of name tags. She found mine and walked us outside onto the front lawn with some other parents.

She smiled brightly. "Susan needs to come with me. She'll be back soon."

I followed her back into the motherhouse with a plastic bag containing my shoes, as my parents found some lawn chairs and sat down. We stood right inside the big entrance doors, and I caught a glimpse of the long corridors stretching out in three directions, and the huge staircase that wound up four stories. I looked up but got dizzy. She told me to follow her upstairs. We stopped at the second floor and she led me into a large empty dorm. At the entrance to the dorm was a table full of plastic bags. She looked through them and found my name on one.

"In here," she said briskly, pointing to a small area with a bed. She handed me the bag. As she closed the curtains, she said, "Hand me your old clothes, please, after you change."

I took off my cool silk blue dress. I left on the cotton underwear and white bra, then covered them with a t-shirt and pulled on the heavy black stockings. I tried to hurry, but it wasn't easy pulling and stretching the new clothes. I had trouble gathering up all the heavy black material over my head and then finding the armholes. I finally smoothed out the dress.

"Is the dress fitting alright?" she asked from outside the curtain.

"Yes," I whispered.

I fastened a large plastic belt covered with fabric around my waist. And I still wasn't finished!

"Are you ready?" she asked impatiently.

"Yes," I answered again.

"I'll help you with the rest," she said as she pulled open the curtains.

She helped me with the short black cape, fastened in the front, on top of the black habit. I put on a black veil lined with white material, my hair poking out from the side.

"You can sit on the bed to put your shoes on." The bed was squishy and soft. I took the old lady shoes that weighed a couple of pounds each and put them on, trying not to think about actually wearing them every day for the rest of my life. I pushed myself up and out of the bed, feeling like I was bundled up to play in the snow, but already dripping sweat from the heat and humidity.

S. Philippa put my clothes and extra bag in the same plastic bag, taking up a lot less room than the ones I had just put on, and handed them to me. She didn't even glance at me but turned and left. I followed, loud in my new footwear.

We went out to the main door and she turned to me, "You can spend some time with your parents now." I went out to where Mom and Dad were waiting with the other parents. I was embarrassed, but one by one, we were all appearing out on the lawn, looking equally ridiculous. I handed my mom the plastic bag with my now useless clothes.

I knew I looked silly in this outfit. I was embarrassed for my parents to see me like this. I felt odd, but proud of my decision. It was my own decision, and I was excited about the possibilities of this new life.

A red-faced older nun, round and nervous, came up to me and my parents.

"Oh, and who is this?" she asked me in a high, shrill voice, but still dripping with honey. She squinted at my name tag.

"I'm Susan, and these are my parents."

She shook my mom and dad's hands.

"I'm Sister Beatrice, the postulant mistress. I'll be in charge of all these wonderful girls this year." Her eyes were quickly moving on to the next group.

"It was so nice..." She turned away, walking toward another group of parents with their daughter. "...to meet you.". I felt embarrassed at her abruptness, but she did have a lot of families to meet.

My mom and dad looked increasingly uncomfortable and I found it difficult to keep the conversation going. Another family came and asked if they could sit next to us in the circle of chairs. Their daughter, Julie, looked as awkward and hot in her new clothes as I did in mine.

All of us as first-year students, instead of being called freshmen, were called postulants. We would be taking regular college courses and studying to be sisters at the same time. Sister Beatrice would be in charge of our hour-long instructions every day, but more than that, she was going to be our guide and caretaker for the entire year, teaching us everything we needed to know about being sisters in this particular order. I wasn't sure what she would be teaching us, but I hoped she'd be nicer than she seemed to be.

The class before us had over sixty students, but the number dropped to thirty-two for ours. Someone whispered that it was because we had psychological testing, but I don't remember much more on my application than a few questions about why we wanted to join.

A handbell rang and many of the postulants started to get up and walk into the building. My parents and I said our goodbyes quickly and hugged. I loved them dearly, but we had run out of things to say.

Mom said, "No tears now. Matterns don't cry. Besides, we'll see you soon." I think she said that to make herself feel better. My dad didn't know what to say but smiled and mumbled something about my being happy. We weren't a demonstrative family. Besides, I would see them in a month, on our first visiting day.

As I climbed up those twenty-five steps, carefully holding up my heavy wool skirts so I wouldn't trip, the building looked like a huge brick prison. I brushed that thought away quickly like an annoying fly. It was the start of my exciting new life!

I was the last one in, and as Sister Philippa closed the massive wooden door behind me, the sunlight disappeared.

Chapter 4
Evening of Day One

We were herded into a large room filled with wooden desks. Each desk had folded paper name tags on them. I looked for my name and sat down. When we were all seated, chattering to our friends, Sister Beatrice called out loudly, "Quiet now, postulants. No more talking. Sister Philippa will take you to your dorms. We have thirty minutes before dinner."

S. Phillipa then led the way, gliding quietly. The rest of us clomped noisily behind her. Up the large wooden stairs, all of us had to lift our serge skirts for the first time, trying not to trip. We made it to the fourth floor without any serious injuries, and only a few bruises.

"Everyone gather around me, please."

We stood outside the large dormitories.

"I'm going to call your names. If you are called, follow me. Hamilton, Emma. Wells, Pamela. Bishon, Juliette." And at least twenty more names.

"The rest of you wait here." I stood sweating. None of us said anything. I smelled some lingering perfume, a cloying odor in the heat, and a few of us scratched at their hot serge. The waiting seemed to take forever.

I heard her shoes first. Then she called nine more names. They went off to the second dorm. There were only three of us left. Had she forgotten about us?

She finally returned. "You three, come with me."

We walked into a small dorm at the end of the corridor.

"Lilian, you have the first bed. Mary Jo, the second, and Susan, back here by the window." My cubicle, she called it a "cell," had a dresser and a twin bed, with a simple cotton bedspread, white of course, and a pillow. The cells were separated by long tan curtains that hung from metal rods just like in hospitals. On the bed was a plastic bag with a white cotton nightgown, a white robe, a washcloth, soap, a toothbrush and toothpaste.

S. Phillipa left, her job finished. We had a half hour to relax. I pulled up my heavy skirts and climbed on the bed, looking

24

out the windows. I heard the two other girls opening drawers, even though there wasn't much to put away, but no one said a word.

The window at the head of my bed looked out past the motherhouse grounds to the small city of Lemay. I could see the hot air shimmering above the houses. I opened the old casement window with peeling white paint, but it wouldn't stay up. I'd have to get a ruler or a book to hold it open. The window at my side looked out to a large courtyard below; a few cars were parked there. Across from it was the chapel. The stained- glass windows almost blinded me with the sunlight reflecting off of them. I felt good about being on the end by the windows. I would hate the closed-in feeling of the other cubicles. I checked my watch. It was four-thirty already--time to go downstairs. The other two girls were gone. They had left without saying a word.

"Oh well," I thought. "They don't know me at all. Why would they wait for me? But it would have been nice if they had said something."

I walked slowly down the three long flights of stairs, holding tightly to the polished wooden handrails. I couldn't even see my feet, so I had to feel for each step. I didn't want to trip and fall on my very first day. That would have been embarrassing.

Everything was so clean and shining. I didn't know yet that the postulants would be responsible for keeping it that way. I saw a few postulants going down the stairs on the third floor and followed them. When we reached the basement, I ran my hand along the thick white-plastered walls. It was much cooler down here. The postulants went into a large room. I hoped they knew where they were going. The sign on the door said "REFECTORY." I figured it must be the dining room, only in Latin. I hoped they called the bathrooms by their correct name.

As I walked inside, I looked around, wondering if I looked as odd as my fellow classmates. Six of us had entered from our high school, and I saw them sitting together at one of the four long wooden tables, with eight chairs at each table.

I spotted Pam. Her dark brown skin almost matched the black dress and veil, and her frizzy brown hair stuck out on all sides of the veil. I always kidded Pam about the color of her hair. I said it was dark brown, and she insisted it was black. We looked at each other and laughed. I hoped I didn't look as silly as she did.

I walked over to the table where they were sitting. Beth, Pam, Nancy, Charlene, and Marianne. I was glad to see familiar faces, a welcome sight in this new and strange world. Beth was nice, but we didn't have much in common. She was short and chubby and was very quiet. She read and studied on the bus as Pam and Nancy and I gossiped and laughed. Pam, Beth, Nancy and I had ridden the same bus to school almost every day in high school, so we knew each other pretty well. We didn't really like Charlene. Pam called her a goody-two shoes. She seemed a little fake with her prayerfulness and holiness. Marianne was like that too. She was eighteen like the rest of us, but she acted like somebody's grandmother. Very prim and proper and judgmental, with her hair always neatly pulled back into a bun, no stray hairs showing. She even looked like a nun in our high school uniforms. As I looked around the room, she and Charlene were the only ones who looked like they belonged in the habit. Pam and I certainly didn't. Neither did Nancy. It seemed like she always ran to catch the bus, papers flying, blouse never tucked in, shoes perpetually untied. Her habit already looked sloppy. I loved her for that.

At our table was one other girl. She told me her name, Juliette, though I didn't catch the last name because she was crying. Her last name sounded French. Through sniffles, she said her parents lived only a few blocks away.

"I'm their only child," she said. as she burst into tears. She told us how homesick she was. Pam looked at me, rolling her eyes. It had only been a half-hour! I felt bad for her, but I wasn't quite sure why she was so emotional so soon.

We passed the cold cuts around the table, and Juliette, who was a little overweight, took five pieces of baloney and three slices of ham, leaving only one of each by the time it got to me. The warm bread was good, though. It tasted and looked homemade, and there was butter and jam to go on it. While we ate, we mostly talked about the afternoon and how strange everything was. How hot the habits were, and how funny we all looked in them. I felt bad for Juliette, since she wasn't part of our group. Even though her parents lived just a few blocks away, they probably wouldn't be seeing much of their little girl. We only had visiting days once a

26

month, and I thought those three blocks might as well have been a hundred miles.

We washed and rinsed our dishes in dishpans that S. Philippa brought to the ends of the tables and reset our places for breakfast the next morning.

After dinner, Sister Beatrice stood up and clinked her water glass loudly with a fork.

"Postulants, postulants, quiet."

It took a few minutes for the noise to disappear.

"We'll be going upstairs for our very first instructions."

We climbed the stairs and walked to the room we'd been in before--the study hall. The desks were old and sturdy, old wood and metal attached to the hardwood floor with large bolts, and the tops opened up so we could store our textbooks inside. I found my desk towards the back of the room and sat down.

Sister Beatrice glided up to the podium in front of the room. I still didn't know what to think of her. She was short and round and over sixty at least. Her face was red, and she held her hands together tightly. She looked as nervous as I felt. Thankfully, her instructions that first evening were simple.

"Postulants! Postulants!" She waited again while we quieted down.

"I'd like to welcome you to the School Sisters of Notre Dame. My name is Sister Beatrice, and I will be in charge of your training as postulants in this order."

She took a breath and I waited anxiously for what she would say next.

"Don't go downstairs alone to take a shower."

"What?" I thought to myself. "That's the very first thing she's telling us? Maybe she's joking."

I smiled at her attempt at humor even though I didn't understand it, but she went on and I realized that she was serious. "There are showers in the dormitories you can use. There are also showers in the basement but never go alone because there might be men down there."

Men? I had no idea what she was talking about. Men weren't allowed in the convent! Were they? Didn't they lock the doors at night?

She continued. "Nine o'clock in the evening begins the Great Silence. It means no talking till after Mass and breakfast the following morning. I repeat--no talking at all unless it's an emergency. We wake up at 4:30 a.m. and go to the chapel where we will have meditation, Mass, and then breakfast. No talking in the bathrooms, ever."

It wasn't an inspirational speech. I was still thinking about men in the convent.

Then she and Sister Philippa handed out our new leather-bound prayer books, containing the Divine Office, which was a series of prayers and psalms said at different times of the day. Since it was evening and we were all tired, Sister Beatrice decided we'd start with Compline, the evening prayer. We went to our very own little postulant's chapel, with just enough pews for us, and were taught how to pray Compline, complete with bowing at the right places. Pam and I stood next to each other and tried not to laugh when we bowed because we were almost touching the rear of the person in front of us. I think a few giggles escaped, but we managed to get to the end of the prayer. We were then told to go to our dorms and get ready for bed, with a warning that the lights would be out at 9:30 p.m. And no talking.

I quietly walked upstairs, surrounded by strangers, and found my little dorm. I took off my stifling hot clothes, put on a thin white robe and waited in line for a shower. It reminded me of the YWCA after swimming practice. I waited for a free sink, brushed my teeth and walked back to the dorm. I had on my regulation white nightgown and lay down in bed, wondering what I had gotten into. No one said a word. I didn't even remember who was next to me in the two other beds. The day had been exciting in a strange way and I was sure it would get better as the days and weeks progressed. The oppressive heat and humidity of St. Louis hung over the city all night, and I grabbed the bar of soap from the top of my dresser and used it to prop open the reluctant window. I was glad I had two windows to catch the slightest breeze. I fell asleep quickly.

Chapter 5
Day 2

I heard the clanging of a bell and for a second didn't know where I was. Then I remembered. The light came on overhead. The air was hot and sticky, and the sky was still black. Outside my window I could see a few stars. I got up, put my thin robe on and went to the bathroom where I washed my face and brushed my teeth. Then I went back to the dorm and tried to get all my clothes on in the right order. I didn't want to be the only postulant with my veil on inside-out, or my dress on backwards. I was finally ready, even without a mirror to help, and walked out of the dorm. My two dorm mates, whoever they were, had left already, so I ran down the stairs as fast as I could in the long skirts. I caught up with a few other postulants on the next landing, so I knew I wasn't too late. We clomped together into the study hall and found our desks. A few minutes later Sister Phillipa told us to stand, and we all rose and lined up to walk down the corridor, through the swinging doors, to the main chapel. We made a tremendous noise--thirty-two pairs of black old lady shoes on the tile floor.

Our debut in front of the other nuns had come. I felt hundreds of eyes on us as we walked up the aisle and filed in the pews. I knelt on the padded kneeler and tried to look like I knew what I was doing. The chapel was prettier than my old church, which had been a converted gymnasium. Our parish had always wanted to build a real church, but no one cared enough to raise the money since the pastor went to Florida for a month every winter, and many people resented Father Bill's yearly vacations with our donation money.

The chapel was sparsely decorated, but its simplicity had no real beauty. It was just plain. There were stained glass windows behind the altar and on both sides of the chapel. They looked like gray glass in the dim light before dawn but were just beginning to get a trace of color as the sun rose.

Most of the nuns were sitting silently, so I sat down. Some of my fellow postulants knelt for a while, and then sat. Everyone just sat there silently, waiting for something. Then I remembered that this was meditation time. I had no idea how to meditate--I didn't even know what the word meant. I hoped that would be one of the first things we'd be taught. It sounded like daydreaming, which I always was told was a waste of time.

I stole a few glances at the postulants around me. The ones to my right and left were sitting quietly and prayerfully, hands in their laps, looking serenely at the altar. I tried not to look at them. I watched the windows get brighter, and the reds and blues were vibrant in the sun. I practiced a few piano pieces in my head, and watched the postulants in front of me, some fidgeting, others quiet with their heads bowed in prayer or sleep.

The hour went surprisingly fast. Then an old priest hobbled out to the altar and started muttering the Mass. He mumbled the words in record time, and it was difficult to tell if the words were English or Latin. I hoped they were in English, and after a few minutes, I realized they were--barely. The church reforms had changed the Latin to English, but I didn't understand one word of that Mass. After Mass we filed back to the refectory to our new assigned places for breakfast. I was starving. At home I'd have a snack every evening with my dad. He'd have a bowl of cereal, and I'd usually join him with my bowl as we watched the last news of the evening. No snacks at night here.

Oatmeal, fruit and big pitchers of milk and orange juice were the centerpieces of the tables. Sister Beatrice read to us from a book of saints while we sat and ate. When we were through, we washed our dishes and put them back at our places for lunch. We still hadn't had a chance to talk.

Then we went upstairs to the study hall for our first real instructions. The past day had been so new and different that I hadn't had time to be homesick. I'd been ready to leave home. I would have left to go to college, so this wasn't that different. Well, it was different. There were no boys or men (except the ones in the basement!), no dating, no prospect of marriage or children. But I wasn't interested in that. I guess I was a late bloomer.

I had gone to an all-girls high school called Rosati-Kain, named after two archbishops. My mother had gone there and believed it was the best school in the city.

I hadn't ever met any boy I liked. I went to the prom with an immature and pimply boy whose name I don't even remember. I

30

had a tremendous crush on Mr. Read, my English teacher at summer school, but it was really just my family and a few friends that I would miss.

Juliette smiled at me. Her eyes were still red, and I felt sorry for her. She didn't seem so immature and silly in the morning. I smiled back at her, and felt bad for her mom and dad, missing their little girl. I was pretty sure my parents were fine. My two sisters had gotten married and left home years before, so they had already experienced daughters leaving home.

I noticed the St. Louis Post Dispatch folded neatly on Sister Beatrice's desk. Good. I loved to read the newspaper and didn't want to lose touch with the world completely. We sat at our big wooden desks and waited for the instructions to begin. Sister Beatrice's voice was high and harsh. The first rule we learned was a greeting. When we saw another nun, even a fellow postulant, we had to say, "Praise to you, Lord Jesus Christ," with our heads bowed. Someone giggled and Sister Beatrice's eyes got hard and small.

"This is nothing to laugh about, postulants. We're going to practice this until you say it correctly."

We had to say, "Praise to you Lord Jesus Christ" to the person next to us and they had to say, "Now and forever, Amen," and then we did it the other way around till we got really sick of saying it. I felt like we were in kindergarten. I was sitting next to a girl called Mary Jo and she took it very seriously, especially after the rude postulant had laughed. I always thought "hello" worked pretty well, but apparently I was wrong.

We, or rather, Sister Beatrice, talked about silence and prayers and getting dressed and studying until it was almost nine o'clock. At least there was no more talk about men in the showers. Then she passed out our college schedules. Not only were we learning to be nuns, we were studying to be teachers, and we were going to an accredited college attached to the motherhouse just for us nuns. She mentioned that we should read the newspaper every day to keep up with current events. But a degree and teaching credential seemed a long way off that first morning.

I looked at my schedule. I had Freshman English, World Literature for English majors, piano, music theory, math, PE, health and theology. It was 20 units plus learning how to be a nun. I hoped my teachers would be good. I had disappointed my parents with their hopes that I would go to a good college. My sisters had gone to secretarial school and I was their last hope of a college-educated daughter. I wanted to prove that I had made the right decision.

Most of the postulants went immediately to their first class. Pam and I realized we didn't start class until 10:30 so we walked up to Sister Beatrice's desk and I picked up the newspaper.

Chapter 6
No News is Good News

As soon as I picked up the newspaper, I knew something was wrong. Some of the pages were hanging out at odd angles. I looked at the front page. Where there should have been headlines there were big gaping holes. Someone had taken scissors and cut out at least half the articles. I opened up the paper. All the pages were cut to pieces.

It had probably taken an hour to go through the paper and make it presentable for our young virgin minds. I looked at Pam and she looked at me. We didn't say anything, and I folded the newspaper as best I could and set it back on Sister Beatrice's desk. Pam and I walked quietly out of the study hall. Halfway down the hall, out of sight of Sister Beatrice, we couldn't hold our laughter in any longer.

"Did you see that?" I finally got the words out.

"Shredded paper for breakfast!" Pam whispered, and we both laughed again.

"Do you think they do that all the time?" I asked her.

"You bet they do. I guess we've gotten ourselves in for something, haven't we?"

We headed down the hall to the college building, still talking and laughing. Pam shook her head slowly. "Girl, I'm going to have my parents bring me all the newspapers for the entire month on visiting day, especially the comics."

"I just can't believe it," I kept saying over and over.

It wasn't like we could go out to buy a newspaper. We were stuck with no money and no transportation. And not a television in sight. Pam and I reached the end of the corridor and we headed in what we hoped was the right direction for our separate classes. At least we could laugh about it.

Every day for the next four years, I read a newspaper that had very few articles in it. Sometimes we could watch the one television in a parlor during our hour of recreation in the evenings, so we didn't miss out on everything, just most of everything.

What did they cut out of the paper? I don't know. I just know what they left in. But I'm sure they cut out everything related to sex. That was the big topic that had to be scissored out every morning.

The Catholic Church always had a problem with sexuality. Ignoring it was usually the best approach. Sins of sexuality were always worse than any other sins. The church could put up with intolerance and hatred, treating your neighbor badly, lying, racism, almost anything that was morally reprehensible, but having sex with someone you weren't married to was the worst sin of all.

Seeing the paper in shreds was funny that first morning, even though I should have seen the writing on the wall. But that had been snipped away too.

Chapter 7
Motherhouse

We went down to the basement that first week to the trunk
room, which resembled the pictures I'd seen in history books of the
catacombs of Rome. Long narrow tunnels, lit by Edison light bulbs
strung on wires. It could have been a scene out of an old horror
movie or a potential crime scene. Our trunks were stored there, as
well as the trunks of the other three hundred or so nuns in the
motherhouse. The floor was dirt. The dust was in layers on many
of the trunks. I wondered if the nuns had left, or just died. No one
wanted to go down there alone. Not only was the entire weight of
the four-story building on top of us, but there were S. Beatrice's
warnings about men. Going down there at night was unthinkable.
Luckily the only things in our trunks were extra stockings and slips
and underwear, not things we'd ever need in an emergency.

The motherhouse was as large as a small town. It was built
in the late nineteenth century for an era where nuns were thriving
and becoming a major part of the educational system of the United
States. From the outside, the motherhouse was a four-story brick
building, solid like the German nun who had founded the order,
but to me, it was a magical place. When I first walked through
those massive carved doors, it seemed like a huge castle. It was
missing the moat, the romance, and the Prince Charming, but it
was still exciting and mysterious. A lot of the mystery came from
the forbidden sections. We as postulants were only allowed in a
small section of the motherhouse until two years had passed and
we took our vows. I snuck a look down the forbidden corridor
when the doors were open by the Big Chapel. Each floor had most
of the area off limits to us. The corridors looked disappointingly
similar to the one I cleaned every morning. But it was the sheer
size of the motherhouse that impressed me, coming from such a
small house. I had come from a tiny seven hundred square-foot
house where I could stand in the center hall, walk ten steps in any
direction, and be at the corners. The three of us girls slept in one of
the two bedrooms, our beds so close together they were touching. I
wasn't prepared for the tremendous size of this building.

There were parlors with big, overstuffed couches with

green velvet fabric that turned different colors as you moved your hand back and forth, and offices where sisters with horn-rimmed glasses worked on finances and missions in far-away countries.

A restaurant-sized kitchen was able to provide food for over three or four hundred sisters. Huge pots boiled on the stoves all day and nuns bustled around cooking, pulling pans from industrial sized ovens. Younger sisters cleaned, swept and polished the kitchen every evening after dinner. It gleamed at night. Stainless steel ovens and refrigerators shone like mirrors, reflecting the courtyard lights outside the windows. The bakery--we even had our own bakery--smelled like fresh bread all morning, and metal carts with squeaky wheels lined the basement hallways waiting for sisters to push the food down the long corridors to the various dining rooms.

On the second and third floors were classrooms with high wood-framed windows looking out to the huge oak trees on the green lawns. Many private but small bedrooms belonged to the nuns who lived in the motherhouse. A chapel the size of a small church dominated the center of the building, towering over two stories, and at night the shadows from the candles on the altar made strange and flickering images on the walls and high ceilings. We even had our own laundry. It had gleaming silver washers and huge industrial rollers that dried and spit out steaming sheets every few seconds. We had to work there once a week. There was an infirmary for the elderly and sick nuns with nursing sisters to take care of them. You could probably spend the entire four years in the motherhouse without ever leaving, except for the occasional doctor or dentist appointment.

A college was connected to the motherhouse by an enclosed bridge that doubled as our "rosary" bridge. Our fully accredited college housed departments of music, art, English, science, languages, and a three-story library.

There were tiny doors, closed and locked, that seemed to lead to nowhere. I told my young niece during a visit that someone lived behind the doors, and I had no idea that she believed for years afterwards that tiny people, perhaps elves, inhabited the convent with us.

We had access to the high school's basketball court and

gymnasium, which didn't interest me at all, since we got plenty of exercise walking from our end of the motherhouse to the college and back many times a day, not to mention the four flights of stairs.

If someone wanted to get lost in the motherhouse, it would have been easy to hide. Except that we had a large blackboard in the corridor outside our study hall with all our names on it. And even though the order hadn't discovered alarm clocks--we were awakened every morning by a large brass bell--they had discovered magnets. We each had a round colored magnet that we moved to whatever part of the building we were in so we could be found in an emergency.

Although the roof was off limits, I could hardly wait to go up there someday with some brave soul who cared as little about the rules as I did. A few friends and I found a way to get out on the roof of the motherhouse early in our first year. I didn't mark that with my magnet! We weren't away from the building, but it gave me a sense of freedom to be out there above the world, gazing out to the river and the city beyond. The gently sloping roof was just dangerous and forbidden enough to be exciting. The bell in the tower rang the Angelus at noon and evening, and finding the little door was all we needed to climb up to the tower and on to the roof.

That first year, I got to know the motherhouse much better than I got to know God. He remained elusive, whereas I learned every accessible part of the huge building. She comforted me at times, other times she scared me. Full of nooks and crannies, unused parlors and classrooms, statues of Mary and Jesus and the saints strewn through the corridors, with little votive candles and kneelers in case someone wanted to say an impromptu prayer. Forbidden places were behind the closed doors, waiting for us to be older or blessed enough to see them.

The motherhouse had a presence of her own; a living, breathing entity who was always watching me; sometimes frightening, sometimes comforting. In contrast to many of the nuns that lived in her, her personality was varied and powerful. Sometimes I felt that if everyone were magically gone, she would still be there watching in mute defiance of the world. She would never go away, and no matter how the winds of change and age battered her, she would remain the same forever.

Chapter 8
Homesick

I was never homesick like Juliette. I don't know how she found the time for it. We were busy from morning till night. We had to learn so much those first few months.

We had to learn how to get dressed, how to put all our clothes on in the right order and get down to the chapel by five am for meditation. I still had no idea how to meditate and kept hoping I would learn, but no one ever said a word about it. We just sat there for an hour every morning trying to stay awake.

I had an exceptional memory for music so I'd listen to symphonies and practice piano pieces and concertos in my head. Many years later I learned that wasn't a waste of time, that practicing in my head was just about as good as the real thing. I didn't know it then. It was just a way to pass the time.

We had to sit through a boring Mass, the ancient priest mumbling the unintelligible words. Never a sermon, though. The elderly priests didn't have enough energy for that, thank God. Priests in the diocese were usually assigned to a parish, but the retired priests still had to say Mass every day, or at least were encouraged to do so. That's why we always got the retired priests at the motherhouse. We never even got sermons on Sunday. We got enough sermons from Sister Beatrice during the week.

We even had to learn breakfast; how to sit, eat, ask for food without speaking, and listen to someone drone on about the life of some dead saint. After that, we had a half hour to walk around the building where we could finally talk.

After our walk around the building every morning, we listened to instructions from S. Beatrice. Every morning we heard about the importance of some very unimportant thing, like why the Great Silence was so important, a lot of pep talks about how nuns had followed these same rules for centuries, and how to become good, holy women. We went to our classes, then met back together for lunch in silence. We had more prayers, then classes until our 3 pm cleaning. Everyone got a different cleaning assignment. We only had to clean our section of the building, since we weren't allowed in the main part of the motherhouse where the real nuns lived.

Some unlucky ones had to clean the toilets and showers. One person had to get up a half-hour early and be ready at 4:30 a.m. in the main corridor to ring the large hand bell, which would wake everyone up in that area of the motherhouse.

I'm glad I never got that duty. I wouldn't have been able to sleep for fear of not waking up in time, even with an alarm. And yes, there was adequate technology for all of us to have alarm clocks. I don't remember questioning why we had to be awakened by an ancient hand-held brass bell. It was just the way it had always been done, like so many other things.

I cleaned the main hall, from the postulant's wing to the swinging doors that led to the restricted part of the motherhouse. I swept and dusted it every day and mopped it every other day. Starting at one end of the long corridor, I pushed the broom past the parlors and offices on the main floor, all the way down to the large grandfather clock that said Tempus Fugit. I also got to clean the stairway up to the second floor. That sounds easy, but each carved wooden post had to be carefully dusted. Sister Phillipa would come by with her white gloves to discover even the tiniest particle of dust. If her gloves were dusty I would be called into the office and told that I was lazy, incompetent, or a host of other personal failings that didn't have anything to do with dusting, as far as I could tell.

We prayed the rosary at 3:30 every afternoon, walking back and forth across the indoor bridge between the motherhouse and the college. The rosary is a repetitive prayer consisting of many Hail Marys and Our Fathers and as you pray them you move your hands over beads to keep track of how many you've said. It's very meditative to be so repetitious. While you say the prayers by rote, you're supposed to be thinking about the great mysteries of Catholicism, like the Nativity, the Resurrection, the Assumption of Mary, and many others.

A lot of the postulants looked down at the floor while they murmured the prayers, but I always tried to look heavenward. There were over four hundred acoustic tiles on the ceiling. I counted them often, and there were lots of little holes in the tiles that had interesting patterns, kind of like constellations, only not as

40

beautiful. I don't think I got much out of saying the rosary.

I also practiced the piano every day. I'd walk over to the music department, open the door to a practice room, and sit for an hour by myself, practicing pieces by Bach, Ravel or Chopin.

Practicing was part of my real education for the first time in my life. All my life playing the piano had been an extracurricular activity, something I made time for because I loved it.

Now I could love it and get credit for it. I was free to be myself during those practice times, the person I had always been. Not the fake nun who followed all the rules and tried hard to fit in. Music became my hour of daily freedom.

I'd joined the convent to be helpful to the world, but I was completely cut off from it. I had joined so I could discover who God really was but I hadn't seen anything of God yet. Just restrictions and regulations and silence and useless meditations and boring instructions from Sister Beatrice.

We had recreation after dinner. It would have been a wonderful time for the thirty-two of us to socialize and get to know each other. We were supposed to be building community but we didn't get more than an hour every day to talk. We played volleyball often, and yes, the thirty-two of us on a volleyball court with long skirts and big shoes and veils flying was as funny as it sounds. Sometimes we danced folk dances. We were told that we would have to teach folk dancing to young children someday. I wasn't sure when that would happen, since I would be a high school English and music teacher, but we had to learn anyway. There were folk dances from many different countries which I found vaguely interesting. Then when "recreation" was over we studied for two hours till nine pm, when we had a half hour to get ready for bed. Lights were out at 9:30, followed by silence until the next morning.

We were busy from morning to night, yet without any discernable purpose. I had to remind myself to be patient.

Someday we would understand the purpose of all these rules. That's what we were told. Generations of sisters had come closer to God through silence and meditation, rules taught us obedience, and all the regulations would build our characters and prepare us for the future.

Just because I couldn't see the benefits didn't mean they didn't exist, but they floated constantly out of my reach. Even though life was strange and different, I really hoped I was doing the right thing. And I wasn't about to give up after a few months. I wasn't about to admit defeat--to my parents, my friends, or myself.

As I lay in bed at night, my body was exhausted and my mind was filled with what everyone was telling me. The Catholic Church had its overwhelming structures and rules on how to be a "good Christian." Then the convent added layer upon layer of additional directions and regulations. The idea of "helping people" seemed lost in the shuffle. No one ever mentioned that we were learning how to help others. The prayers, the chores, the classwork and homework filled in the last sections of my brain, and I was too tired to even think.

As I got older, I read that this is what they do in cults--keep people busy all day, tire them out physically, and fill their heads with propaganda. At 9:00 every night, I climbed silently up to the dorm where I took off all my clothes, one strange piece at a time. Some nights I felt like I was shedding not only the uncomfortable, odd clothes, but also the strangeness and restrictions of this new life. I crawled into bed still blanketed by the rules. By then I would be asleep.

Chapter 9
The Basement

I turned off the shower in the basement, and silence settled around me. When I had started my shower, there were a few classmates in the other stalls nearby. I could see the fog of the rising steam and feel the moist air. Someone hummed a Beatle's tune and a hair dryer's insistent whine rose over the running water, but now as I turned the water off, there was no sound at all. I hoped that everyone hadn't left. I dried quickly as the cold crept over my body, pulled my thin white robe tightly around me, gathered up my clothes, and padded out into the brightly lit shower room.

Despite the rule of silence, I squeaked out, "Is anyone here?"

My voice echoed off the wet tile walls and faded away. No one answered. I asked again, just to make sure. Silence. I was completely alone. I clicked off the lights and stood mutely in the complete darkness. The massive motherhouse breathed around me.

Hundreds of sisters lived in the motherhouse, but now for the first time in months, there was no one around me. All of S. Beatrice's warnings flooded back to me. "Never go down to the basement showers alone at night. There could be MEN down there." I'd laughed at the time, imagining some incredibly stupid man waiting all day in the dark corridors of the motherhouse basement for some poor postulant to take a shower. There had to be an easier way, even for the most desperate sexual pervert. Now the warning seemed to make sense.

I had turned off the light switch but kept my hand on it, just in case, wondering how I was going to find my way down the pitch-black corridor to the elevator at the end of the long hall. I peered down the corridor and as my eyes adjusted, I could finally make out a pale light from the elevator shaft. And gradually I could see the faint outlines of the high windows recessed in the thick plastered walls.

I held my breath and tiptoed down the hall.

Every time I gingerly placed my bare foot on the concrete, I expected to feel a squirming cockroach under my toes. I would

43

scream if that happened, and I wouldn't be at all concerned about breaking the rule of silence. Suddenly it seemed very likely that there were men waiting down here, lining the dark corridor. I ran faster, feeling like someone was watching me, ready to step out and grab me. I made it to the elevator and pressed the one red button repeatedly.

I had wished many times to have some time alone, but not like this. I felt the dark heavy walls closing in one me as I waited for my only way out. I could hear the creaking and sighing of the ancient Otis elevator as the chains clanked. Gradually it came into view and finally rested on the concrete slab.

The elevator was reserved for the elderly nuns who couldn't walk up and down the stairs. We were allowed to use it at night to take showers in the basement. They probably really didn't want the students to use it but decided it was better than having us wandering the halls and staircases in our white nightgowns and thin robes, looking like ghosts.

I grabbed the iron handle and pushed back the grate. The light was comforting. I practically leapt inside and hurriedly pulled the grate closed, feeling a sense of triumph, then pushed the button for the fourth floor. The elevator creaked upwards; I could see the darkness of the first floor, then the wooden flooring and the steel reinforcements in between the floors, then the darkness of the second floor. I simultaneously wished it would go faster and was amazed that it worked at all. As the elevator clanked its way upwards, I imagined S. Beatrice standing at the elevator door, hands on hips, waiting for me at each floor.

The elevator made it to the fourth floor, and I got out quickly. The familiar darkness of this corridor was warm and cozy in contrast to the cold basement. I shivered at the thought of it. That was the last time I'd go down there without a companion whom I was sure would wait for me.

44

Chapter 10
Sex Education

S. Beatrice looked unusually serious as she stepped up to the podium for our morning instructions.

"Good morning, postulants."

"Good morning," a few of us replied softly. I wondered if I could leave my English book open and glance at it during instructions. I decided against it and closed it reluctantly.

"Let's try that again, postulants."

This time we yelled, "Good morning!" like we were in grade school. I sat with my hands folded, giving her my complete attention, except for watching the postulants around me without moving my head, noticing the trees blowing outside the window and glancing at a few cracks on the walls and ceilings.

She paused. "You need to be friends with all the members of our little community. That is the secret to building community. And we have to start with our own little group, and then expand to all our sisters, and then the whole world. I've started to see some disturbing signs that don't contribute to community, and I need to speak to you about this."

I started listening. This wasn't going to be about some dead saint, thank God. Friendship was really important to me and I wondered what guidance, if any, she would have. I still held out a little hope that she might have some insights, although that was fading with each day.

"We naturally will be drawn to certain people and want to spend more time with them, but postulants, we cannot neglect other members of the community. We must be careful to spend time with everyone and not form Particular Friendships with anyone."

She took a deep breath. "I'm going to tell you a story. A story to warn you about the dangers of Particular Friendships. A few years ago, a sister was walking down the hall late at night, past midnight. She had been taking care of a sick sister and was returning to her room. She stopped to pray at the statue of Mary, the one right down the hall. As she knelt down and started to pray, she heard whispering. She got up and looked behind the statue and there were two postulants behind the statue!"

She paused, speechless, unable to continue for a full minute.

After giving us time to try to figure out what she was talking about, she cleared her throat and her face seemed to get redder than it already was.

"Postulants, we must be very careful not to form "these kinds" of friendships. If you talk to one person during recreation, make sure you spend time with a different person the next evening. That way you will make sure that you never fall into the danger of Particular Friendships!"

And the thankfully short instruction period was over--just like that. It certainly gave me a lot to think about--like what in the hell was she talking about? I certainly didn't see any danger in talking to someone behind a statue. What else could they possibly be doing?

I entered the convent in 1966, but grew up in the 50's, when "Leave it to Beaver" and "Father Knows Best" were the popular shows, and a woman's role was clear--be subservient to your husband, who knows a lot more than you do.

Sex education was not a popular topic. There might have been some classes about it in public schools, but there sure weren't any in Catholic schools.

The first I ever thought or heard about sex was in fourth grade. I remember Jerry, a fellow fourth grader, standing around with a group of boys, laughing hysterically at something, and calling out to us girls to look up "intercourse" in the dictionary. And then they whispered and laughed again even harder.

We girls stood off in our group, talking about how ridiculously immature they were, but I'll bet I wasn't the only one who went home and looked the word up--only to be pretty disappointed. It was conversation between people and only the third definition mentioned it had something to do with sex. But I wasn't sure what they were laughing at. At that time, I still had no idea what "sexual intercourse" even was.

I must have been in 7th or 8th grade when, as I was putting away some laundry in my parent's bedroom, I discovered a large book about sex--with drawings!

I had just enough time to see how "it" worked, to be very disgusted with anyone doing "it", especially my parents, and to put the book away quickly but carefully as my mom came in the front door from grocery shopping. The next time I looked for the book, it had mysteriously disappeared.

I attended an all-girls high school and looking at the male specimens that travelled on the bus morning and evening, from the workers to the high school students, pimples and all, I wasn't very impressed or interested in doing "it" with any of them!

The only man I adored was my 40ish English teacher in summer school, and although I daydreamed about a life with him, my dreams never got beyond a chaste kiss, or saving him from some tragic accident, and nursing him back to health.

I was never kissed in high school. My prom date didn't even try. I do remember that he wanted to hold my hand when we went to see "My Fair Lady," my only other date with him after the prom, but his hand was sweaty and I was much more impressed with Rex Harrison.

Not only did I know nothing about heterosexual sex, I knew even less, if that's possible, about gays and lesbians. I didn't even know that Liberace was gay. I just knew that I hated him with a passion because I felt he made a mockery of the piano-- something that was very important to me. It was all a show to him, and he valued his bank account more than music. He even said that in an interview. Someone mentioned to me in high school that Rudolf Nureyev might be gay and I was shocked that they could even think such a thing. What a horrible thing to say about someone, and although I knew that it meant a man loved another man, I never got much further in my mind than it was terribly wrong, and against everything that the Catholic church believed in. I wasn't really sure why. So when S. Beatrice attempted some education about sexual matters, I was not only completely unprepared, but I also had no idea what she was talking about. I'm not too sure she did either.

After S. Beatrice's short and vague instruction period, recreation time the following week was very confusing. Everyone tried to talk to someone that they had never talked to before. Our normal groups were completely disrupted, and we were afraid to be with our friends or even talk to them two times in a row.

Luckily that didn't last too long, and we got back to a semi-normal kind of relationship with the other postulants. But after that I was afraid of being seen with the same person too often. It seemed paranoid, and I thought there had to be better ways of instilling community spirit in us than making us feel guilty about our friendships.

After a few weeks I forgot about Particular Friendships, although I always did wonder what those postulants were doing behind that statue!

Chapter 11
The Bouncing Ball

The chapel was deathly quiet as the ancient priest held up the wafer of bread, intoning the words, "This is my Body." The Consecration is the holiest part of the Mass, where the bread and wine are, quite literally, transformed into the Body and Blood of Christ.

The bleary, half-opened eyes of four hundred nuns watched the priest as he performed the ancient ritual. Mine should have been, but instead I looked at the stained-glass windows. My eyes were always drawn to them, the only things of beauty in the chapel, and especially since we were sitting right under them.

We postulants sat in the upstairs loft on the right side of the chapel, so we had a birds-eye view of not only the windows, but the altar below, and part of the congregation. I happened to be in the front row that morning; Pam was to my left, then Trish, and Margaret at the end of the row. We were all kneeling, our hands prayerfully folded together.

Instead of thinking about the miracle of the Consecration, which happened every day at Mass and was getting pretty old, I glanced at my fellow postulants.

Margaret was probably my least favorite classmate. She was eighteen like the rest of us but acted like she was going on fifty. She wore her hair tightly in a bun, even under her veil, and when she smiled it was like something hurt inside, probably her hair. I never talked much to her because it was like talking to a teacher. Her small lips were always tightly pressed together, her head down and her eyes cast demurely at the floor, as if that's what a good nun should be looking at. She was the first in chapel and the last to leave. S. Beatrice thought she was a wonderful example for the rest of us.

Trish was next to her. She stared devoutly at the altar and looked particularly holy this morning, which was unusual. Suddenly I saw her lean forward slightly. She clutched her rosary in one hand, and with her right hand fished something out of her large skirt pocket. She brought her hand nonchalantly up to the rail, her head bowed in prayer. I saw something fall from her hand.

Then she refolded her hands.

A small yellow neon ball fell slowly from the loft, as if suspended in the heavy morning air. I watched in horror and then delight as it fell down to the green tile floor directly to the right of the altar. I couldn't believe Trish had done this.

Actually, I could. Trish was from Teutopolis, a small farm town in Illinois. She was wild, and not just by convent standards, which were pretty low. She seemed better suited to raising hell with her brothers, cow-tipping on Saturday nights, and getting drunk on Southern Comfort, which she boasted about constantly. She had a perpetual smirk on her face and was always looking for trouble. Some of us had seen the super ball before. She had gotten it from one of her younger brothers last visiting day. Why she had joined the convent was a mystery since she didn't seem interested in following any of the rules.

The ball bounced high, almost as high as the loft, leaving a trail of neon yellow, and soared in a great arc in front of the sleepy nuns. I could see a few veils moving sideways in the pews below, one by one, as they caught sight of the ball. I turned further to see their faces.

The nuns in the main chapel usually wore masks of pleasantness and Christian kindness, but the bland looks were slowly replaced by furrowed brows, wide-eyed shock, and complete dismay at the sacrilege taking place before their eyes.

Inside, nervous laughter trapped beneath two months of holiness bubbled up to the surface. Trish had picked the holiest part of the Mass for maximum effect. I didn't dare laugh, not with S. Beatrice sitting directly behind us. I glanced at Pam next to me. Her dark skin couldn't hide the tears escaping from her eyes as she struggled not to laugh. She looked down at her lap. She couldn't get in any more trouble. Trouble seemed to follow her.

The ball seemed to glide even higher on its second bounce. I couldn't believe how high it soared. It really was a "super ball." Now it came down in front of the priest behind the communion rail. The priest stopped mumbling, his head jerking up abruptly as he followed arc of the ball. He caught himself then, and wearily knelt on one knee after he said the words of the Consecration.

By this time, as the ball hit the floor and bounced a third

50

time, almost all the eyes in the chapel were off the priest and on the ball.

I didn't dare look over at Juliette, next to me on my right. She was probably hoping that S. Beatrice wouldn't think it was her who had caused the trouble. Juliette was a large girl with white pasty skin and black hair, and she could never do anything right, from how she recited her prayers to how she wore her veil or tied her shoes. She still froze in terror when S. Beatrice asked her anything. She had nothing to do with the ball but would have probably cried and confessed if S. Beatrice had accused her.

Angela sat by the wall. She was fun and mischievous and would have joined any adventure if she had been invited, but wouldn't embarrass herself and all of the postulants by doing this. She was a follower, not a leader. Right now she was watching the ball, wide-eyed and trying not to smile.

I stared at my lap and fingered my rosary beads, trying to think of anything but the bouncing ball. It was hard to keep from laughing, since I was starting to hear laughter all around me. I thought about the Mass. That didn't help. I thought about how much trouble we were all going to be in. That helped a little.

I just had to look. The ball had made four great arcs in front of the chapel, and as it shot upwards toward the far wall, a two hundred-fifty-pound nun stood up in the front pew. With a terrible scowl on her face, and an effortless leap for someone her size, she reached high in the air, seized the ball like a major league outfielder and held it tightly. As she turned, she gave a scathing look in our direction, and the ball disappeared in her voluminous black skirts. We never saw it again.

I heard noises like someone being strangled behind me, but realized it was just stifled laughter from the rest of the postulants in the loft. I could feel S. Beatrice's eyes bore into the six of us in the front pew, staring at our backs with her small beady eyes, trying to figure out who had dropped the ball. I felt she could look right through me.

I knew that I was safe. She would never think it was me. I was quiet and soft-spoken. She didn't know what I really thought.

A few minutes later it was time for Communion. We had to stifle our laughter, stand up, turn, and walk directly past S.

Beatrice. She stared at each one of us, trying to see guilt in our slightest facial twitch. She was trying to turn us from immature worldly teenagers into compliant, obedient nuns. She had a lot of work to do.

When Mass was finally over, we walked in silence down the dark halls to our refectory. We sat through breakfast as usual, listening to the lives of the saints. But the silence that morning was tense and nervous instead of the usual drowsiness. We knew that we'd hear about the ball, sooner or later. We just didn't know when. Breakfast passed without incident. As we stood up to leave, S. Beatrice said with a shaking voice, "Postulants, we will not have our morning walk around the motherhouse. You will go directly to the study hall and we will begin our instructions."

We walked up the wooden stairs and filed into the large study hall where we waited in complete silence. No one felt like laughing anymore.

S. Beatrice came out of her office and walked to the front of the room. She stood with her hands tightly clutching the wooden sides of the podium. Then she removed a handkerchief from somewhere deep inside her black habit and wiped her forehead. She replaced it carefully in her long sleeve. We sat silently.

"Postulants." She waited a full minute for that information to sink in. I was beginning to wonder if she would ever go on. Then she continued, "I have never been more embarrassed and disgraced than I was this morning at Mass. I have taught many classes over the years, and never have I been so disappointed and humiliated as I am today."

Her voice got higher with each sentence. "Your class is a disgrace to this order of the School Sisters of Notre Dame and all the nuns who have gone before you. I thought, yes I did, a few months ago when your class entered, that it was going to be a difficult year. I saw your attitudes and the way you have ignored the tried-and-true rules of this convent. But I had no idea how difficult it would be."

She paused. There wasn't a sound in the room. Then she continued, even louder.

"I can't understand why this has happened. Sister Phillipa and I have tried our hardest to make you understand how serious

52

this life is. I see that all these instructions have been in vain. I do not see the need for further instructions today. I will leave you to meditate on this unfortunate incident for the next hour. I hope you will all seriously reconsider your commitment to religious life. That is all." She turned from the podium and walked sadly across the front of the room to her office.

An hour! We had to just sit here doing nothing? We sat for an hour, not daring to pull out any textbooks or do anything that would make the slightest bit of noise. I thought a lot about the incident, but with no remorse. I had to be careful not to smile for that whole hour. After all, it was pretty hilarious and I hadn't done anything. I wondered who would turn Trish in and how long it would take for her to be thrown out. I looked out the window a lot and practiced my Spanish vocabulary in my head. The hour went by quickly.

Trish wasn't thrown out that day. No one turned her in. I was surprised about that, considering all the holier-than-thou postulants who knew exactly who had dropped the ball. But they never snitched. I don't know why. It took till Halloween when Trish soaped some car windows in the parking lot, and then she was gone.

When Trish got kicked out, it was like she had never existed. There was an empty place at her desk the next morning, but no announcement and no explanation. The only information we got was gossip from those who had heard about the soaping of the car windows. I learned that's how it always was when someone left. Complete silence. No announcements. No explanations. Just rumors and an empty place until the desk was finally taken out.

I don't remember much from all those years of daily instructions on the rules and regulations of the convent--well, actually--I remember nothing. But to this day, the memory of that bouncing yellow ball is as clear in my mind as the morning it happened, and always brings a smile to my lips.

Chapter 12
My Eighth Grade Essay Contest

Most Catholic girls growing up in the 50's and early 60's dreamt about joining the convent at least once or twice, especially my classmates in our Catholic grade school. Not me. By the time I was in eighth grade, that was the very last thing I wanted to do.

The Catholic Church practically shoved the idea of a vocation down our throats. The word "vocation" in the dictionary meant a "call to enter a certain career," but in the Church it meant becoming a priest or nun. Marriage was a distant second and being single was not a vocation at all. It was an unfortunate accident, not something you chose. If you were unlucky enough to be single, you were on your own with no help from the church. No sacrament for you.

Even though both nuns and priests were members of communities of religious life and took vows of poverty, chastity and obedience, nuns were never given the status of clergy in the Church. We were still classified as the laity because we were women. Only priests received the sacrament of ordination, and nuns were always relegated to being very low in the hierarchy of the church.

In order to encourage vocations, the St. Louis archdiocese sponsored a yearly essay contest about vocations. Sister Alberta, my eighth-grade teacher, looking all tightly sewn together in black with only her red face poking out of the top, announced the contest like it was the Pulitzer Prize for literature. I loved to write, but my heart sank at having to write about the one thing I didn't have--a vocation.

I walked the one block home from school that day, kicking rocks along the path, and threw my books down on the kitchen table. My mom was making liver and onions for dinner and the smell permeated our little house. It smelled good to me. My mom wasn't a great cook, but she had a few good meals that she cooked regularly. Roast and potatoes on Sunday, liver and onions at least once a week, but many evenings we went to Steak & Shake or the Italian restaurant for pizza and pasta.

My mom went back to college for the four years I attended

high school, and I don't remember her cooking very much at all. We studied a lot together in the evenings at the kitchen table, and even then, I was impressed that she was breaking the mold of low expectations for women--and getting a good education.

"We have to write a stupid essay on vocations." I paused for a second. "I don't want to be a nun. How am I supposed to write about it?"

My mom didn't even turn around as she flipped the sizzling liver with the spatula. "Well, write about why you don't want to be one."

I took a sip of cold Coke around the ice cubes and thought about it. What a good idea. I'd finish the assignment and turn it in so I wouldn't get an F. Maybe I'd even get a C for effort.

I pulled up a kitchen chair and sat down. "You know, that's a good idea. I mean, we're supposed to tell the truth, right? And the truth is that being a nun is the last thing on earth I want to be."

"Well, then, write whatever you want. They can't expect everyone to have a vocation. And call dad from the basement. Dinner's ready."

My mom was a good enough Catholic but was not infatuated with nuns or priests. I think that's because she taught at my elementary school and had to work with them every day.

I remember one morning she was terribly angry after reading the newspaper, slamming her coffee cup down hard on the grey table.

"Listen to this! The bishop of St. Louis says, and I'm quoting, 'We must pray for more vocations. Our cheap labor supply to our Catholic schools is drying up and we can't afford to hire more teachers.' Cheap labor supply! He's talking about the nuns. How's that for gratitude." My mom never forgot that article and brought it up in our conversations many times.

I spent a few hours on the essay, rewrote it so it was legible, and turned it in. I never gave it another thought.

The winter passed quickly. Spring of eighth grade was a time when we didn't study very much. I had already gotten into a good high school and my classmates and I were just counting the days till school let out for the summer. I had completely forgotten about the essay contest. I sat in class, reading about Bolivia for a country report when the principal's voice crackled on the loudspeaker.

"Girls and boys," she hissed through the white noise of the microphone, "I'm proud to announce that two of our students have won the vocation essay contest of the archdiocese." I listened only out of curiosity. I wondered who it would be. Probably Marjorie, the class darling. She won everything.

"Our winners will participate in a special Mass for Vocations next week at the St. Louis Cathedral where they will receive their awards. Jerry Engels has won honorable mention in the contest. And Susan Mattern has won first place. Congratulations to both of you." And the loudspeaker crackled again and then was silent. Everyone stared at me.

Sister Alberta said in a confused little voice, "That's wonderful. Congratulations to both of you."

I glanced over at Jerry. He looked very pleased with himself. My face felt hot. I didn't know quite where to look so I looked down at my desk. I had never won anything before. And now I had shocked everyone, including myself, by winning the very contest I didn't want to win. Part of me was proud I had won something, but most of me was just plain embarrassed.

The worst part was the following week--walking down the aisle in the huge St. Louis Cathedral with Jerry Engels, like we were getting married or something. He had never even looked or said anything to me in years. Maybe he thought he was too cool for me.

Actually, I knew why Jerry never spoke to me. Years before, in the fourth grade, we had a talent show. Jerry played the piano, like I did, so we both picked a piece to play in front of the class. Jerry got up, bowed, and put his music on the piano. He played a simple second grade piece, which I had played when I was six. Everyone clapped for him. Then it was my turn.

I walked up to the piano. I was very shy, but playing the piano was the one thing I could do beautifully. I sat down and played Maleguena, a piece which was about ten grades more difficult. And I had it all memorized. Everybody clapped loudly when I was finished. Jerry looked down at his hands with a scowl. He was not happy. Maybe that's why he never spoke to me.

56

There were many students from all over the archdiocese at the Cathedral but Jerry and I were at the beginning of the procession since I had won first place. Long concrete steps led up to the massive stone cathedral. We walked through the wooden front doors to the vestibule which was filled with gold mosaics. The St. Louis Cathedral has more mosaics than any other cathedral in the world except St. Mark's in Venice, but the only thing I saw that day was its long aisle that stretched out in front of me. We were so far away that the altar looked tiny. The organ began a prelude and we walked all the way down to the very first pew. My mom was there, looking proud as I walked down the long aisle.

I wondered as I walked to the huge marble altar if I hadn't made myself clear enough in the essay. And then a terrible thought came to me. Maybe they had gotten the wrong person. But no one said anything, and everyone assumed that I was just a few years away from my dream of becoming a nun. I tried to tell everyone I had won the contest on vocations by writing an honest essay about not having a vocation, but I don't think anyone believed me. I finally gave up trying to explain.

And then four years later I joined the convent. I couldn't even explain that to myself.

Chapter 13
Pam and the Cockroaches

I noticed that Pam looked a little pale at breakfast one morning. I tried to catch her eye, but she didn't look up. As we started our walk around the building, I waited for her.

"I'm in so much trouble," Pam whispered quickly.

"Why? What happened?" I was surprised. It was still early in the day. How could she have gotten in trouble already? Although with Pam, I knew it was possible.

"I did something real stupid last night," she looked around to make sure no one else was listening.

"Last night? What do you mean? How could you get into trouble?"

"Well, I needed to go. You know, to the bathroom. So I just got up and went. I didn't put on my robe or anything. I knew I wouldn't run into S. Beatrice because she was asleep."

"Oh, no." I could guess what was coming next.

"Well, I finished what I was doing, you know, and I could hear footsteps in the bathroom and then I could see those ugly big shoes and I just knew it was S. Beatrice. I didn't have my robe on or anything to cover my head and I had to think fast."

"So what happened?"

"Well, I decided that if I was sleepwalking, then I couldn't get in any trouble for not being dressed. But I had to show S. Beatrice that I was sleepwalking and I didn't quite know how to do that."

"Oh, no." I couldn't even imagine.

"I walked out of the stall and I started stepping on fake cockroaches."

"You did what?"

"Well, I pretended there were hundreds of cockroaches on the floor and I was trying to kill them. I kept dancing around, stomping on one here and seeing another one there, and I gradually worked my way out of the bathroom and into the hall."

"What did S. Beatrice do?" My mouth stayed open in amazement.

"She just stood there and watched me. I kept up my

stomping and killing the cockroaches because I figured it was working, all the way down the hall and into the dorm until I turned the corner."

"Do you really think it worked?" I asked, hoping that Pam wouldn't get thrown out.

Pam looked at me with her big brown eyes. "I don't think so. I think I'm going to be in a lot of trouble in a few minutes."

Always the optimist, I said, "Well, she hasn't said anything yet. Maybe she won't. Maybe she believed you were sleepwalking."

"I think I'm going to hear about it." Pam looked down at the ground. We'd come almost all the way around the building. I looked at her and suddenly imagined her stomping on the roaches, her thin legs and bare feet doing an incredible dance.

"I wish I could have seen that," I whispered. And then I couldn't help it. I started to laugh.

Pam's mouth twitched slightly, then she giggled. "I was good, girl. I was excellent at killing those cockroaches. And there were hundreds of them."

I couldn't stop laughing and neither could Pam.

"I better laugh now, cause I'm not going to be laughing in a few minutes," she could barely get the words out.

"I know, but whatever made you think of killing cockroaches?" I managed to ask.

"Well, you try just standing there knowing you're in big trouble. You see what ideas you come up with."

We laughed the rest of the way around the building till we got to bakery square. Pam wiped her eyes with her long black sleeve. "How do I look?"

"Like you've been laughing all the way around the building." Pam started to laugh again but stopped and tried to put on a solemn face as we walked up the stairs to instructions.

Pam was right. S. Beatrice didn't even waste a second.

"Postulants," she said in a grave voice, "Last night I was in the fourth-floor lavatory, and I saw a postulant who obviously doesn't think much of the rules of this order."

I didn't dare look at Pam. I just stared at my desk. S. Beatrice continued, "But it was not only that the postulant didn't

59

bother to put her robe on and has no sense of modesty about her body, that was not the worst thing."

She paused for dramatic effect. "The postulant then went on to pretend she was sleepwalking, so that she would not be caught breaking the rules. She obviously thinks I'm very stupid and that I wouldn't realize she was deceiving me. These rules are not for my benefit, postulants, they are for you so that you will grow as sisters of this community." She droned on and on. I stopped listening.

Pam was called into the office for her private consultation with S. Beatrice and emerged a half-hour later into the study hall. She managed to roll her eyes when she looked at me. That was a good sign. Pam wouldn't be kicked out--yet.

I wish videotapes had been invented in 1966 so I could have taped that cockroach dance. I'll bet it was an award-winning performance. S.Beatrice could be a tough critic.

Pam and I met the first week of high school. I had settled into my slightly sticky vinyl bus seat, and pulled out my new World Literature textbook, but mostly I watched out the window. Taking the bus was a new experience for me. My grade school had been one block away from my house. I could actually see it from my back yard, a cruel reminder on weekends and in the summer. Now I would be on the bus for two hours every day to get to and from my new high school.

The bus drove through Jennings in north St. Louis, where the whites lived, past the small arms plant, an old factory from the Second World War, and down Goodfellow Blvd. to Wellston, the black area of town.

The bus wheezed to a stop and the door opened. A girl about my age climbed on with books piled high in her arms. She had on a Rosati-Kain uniform. As she walked down the aisle looking for a seat, I saw the green velvet ribbon on her blouse that showed she was a freshman. I patted the seat next to me and smiled.

Her hair was frizzy and black and she looked like she had run the entire block to catch the bus.

"Hi, I'm Sue."

"Hi there. My name's Pam."

60

"What classes are you taking?"

The ride was filled with, "Who's teaching that?" and "What homeroom are you in?" and worries about the amount of homework we might get. We didn't have time to talk about much else that first day, but we usually took the same bus every day and got a lot of talking in. The only class we had together was speech, which we both decided we hated after the first day.

We got off the bus at Delmar Loop, an actual bus depot where you could wait inside in the winter, if you could stand the musty, urine-scented odor. If it got cold enough, we went inside. We waited for the Lindell bus, which took us by Forest Park and the mansions which faced the park. Even now, with my opinion jaded by California home values, they are still mansions.

And then past the Chase Park Plaza hotel--THE fanciest hotel in all St. Louis--right up to the St. Louis Cathedral. Our school was across the street. I had been in the cathedral to receive my essay award, and it was, and still is one of the most beautiful cathedrals in the United States.

We got out of the bus that first day into crowds of students and made our way into the building. After homeroom, Pam and I went our separate ways to our classes, but it was nice to have made a friend.

We met often after school, because we took the same buses home, and it was awfully nice to have someone with me when the days got cold and dark. Sometimes by the time we caught the bus, the sky was dark already, and the cold rain or snow would have already blanketed the city. We would often go to the little market on the corner, which had a soda fountain. I would order a diet drink, and Pam would get a milkshake because she could never gain any weight. Then we'd walk up a few more blocks to get the Kingshighway bus and ride together, gossiping and chatting, till Pam got off at her stop. I lived about fifteen minutes further north, but never minded the long rides when she was with me.

It's strange to say, but we were never best friends. We were friends, and we liked each other and had fun, but the bus rides were all we did together. I had my best friends at school, and Pam had hers. It had nothing to do with race. I just had other friends that I had more in common with, like music and favorite movies and

61

movie stars.

I was awfully glad, though, when Pam decided to join the convent. She wasn't the kind of religious, prayerful Catholic who always seemed to join. We were both rebels in our small ways. I was very quiet about my rebelliousness--Pam was louder and got in more trouble because of it--but we understood each other in a way that my other classmates didn't.

Even in the convent, we were close, but not "best friends" close. Not the kind of friend I could talk to for hours at a time, although we were there for each other and cared for each other. When we entered, Pam was the only black girl in our class. She was one of two black girls in the entire province, perhaps the whole order.

The girl who had entered the year before Pam was named Charlesetta. She had gone to our high school and was the sweetest person anyone could ever meet. Quiet and demure, she slipped into the nun's habit and the lifestyle very easily. Charlesetta never raised her voice, never got in trouble, and was a model sister.

Pam was no Charlesetta. Pam was in trouble from the day she entered. High school didn't bring out the rebel in Pam, but the convent certainly did.

Sometimes she got into trouble because of her color. That sounds very racist, but it wasn't exactly that. I'm sure that some of the nuns were racist--it was an old German order--but if a group of us postulants were laughing or talking at the wrong time, Pam would be singled out. The older nuns couldn't distinguish between all us white sisters in the same habit, but they could spot Pam easily. A lot got blamed on her that wasn't her fault.

But Pam's knack for getting in trouble went way beyond her color. It was her attitude that bothered our superiors. Fighting for what she believed was right, wanting life to be fair, and trying to understand the meaning of the rules--these were bad attitudes in the convent where obedience was Godlike.

Pam got in lots of trouble for speaking out about injustices and trying to make the nuns more aware of social issues. I wanted to care about social issues but it was hard for me to care about anything but our everyday lives. Going to school, praying, making friends, staying out of trouble, practicing the piano. This was my

62

life, and it was difficult to summon much enthusiasm for anything else.

I admired that Pam cared so much. I just couldn't do it. There were moments of national interest, riots or assassinations or threats of war, and the actual war in Vietnam, that pulled me out of my sheltered existence, but they were few in number.

And then there were the troubles that only Pam could think of, like the cockroaches.

Chapter 14
French 101

I was in a tiny practice room one morning in November, trying to learn "J'eau d'eaux" by Ravel, a tricky but beautiful impressionistic piece. It was harder than I thought, and since my favorite composer was Bach, totally different from what I was used to playing.

The small window of the practice room faced the river, but a large sulfur plant blocked the view. The cold sunlight was streaming in the window as I kept going over a difficult passage.

A knock on the door surprised me. I got up quickly, assuming it was my music teacher. Opening the door, I saw a sister I had never met before. I had seen her though, and knew she was from the Mankato province in Minnesota.

"Excuse me, can I come in and listen to you? My name's Joan." She wasn't much older than I and was quite beautiful. Her blue eyes and reddish lips didn't need any makeup. Most nuns looked washed-out and pale in the habit, but her face was rosy-cheeked and healthy.

"Sure, come in." I was surprised anyone had noticed my playing. She sat on the chair behind me as I played through the piece.

"You play beautifully," she said. "What's the name of that?"

"It's French, J'eu d'eaux" by Ravel," I answered.

"Oh, that means "Fountains in the rain," doesn't it?"

Seeing my surprised look, she said quickly, "I'm a French major. Play more for me."

She sat in the practice room while I practiced. I tried to concentrate but she was full of life and fun comments and we talked as much as I played. I'd be in so much trouble if I were caught. She liked my playing and was fun to talk with. Making friends was more important to me than any rule.

After about fifteen minutes, she got up, "Keep playing. I'll be back. I have to get my friend."

She came back in a few minutes with another sister named Maribeth, her classmate, and introduced us. They pulled in another

64

chair and we talked till I had to be back for lunch.

"Let me know when you're practicing, Sue, and I'll come here instead of the library to study."

I suddenly had a good idea. Outside the practice rooms there was a cupboard built into the wall. Each of us music students had a cubbyhole where we could keep our sheet music. I stopped by every day to get my music and returned it when I was finished practicing.

I turned to Joan and Maribeth. "I can leave a note in here and tell you when I'm practicing. Just check this box here on the right."

Maribeth winked at me with her dark brown eyes. She was Czechoslovakian and had a dark complexion and she smiled with sudden delight. "This is fun. It's so sneaky, something exciting to do in our otherwise boring existence."

I didn't know if she was joking.

"Great," said Joan, nodding her head in agreement. "Intrigue. That's what it is! Let's meet every day. I love it!"

"Sounds good." I turned and walked away quickly, worried about lunch.

"Don't be late," Maribeth called after me.

And so we began a wonderful friendship. They were junior sisters, two years out of the novitiate, and were from the Mankato province up north. They both would be practice teaching soon and then get a teaching assignment back in Minnesota.

I left notes for Joan and Maribeth. They listed my practice times only. I never signed them because I was too afraid of being caught. Sometimes Maribeth would visit, sometimes it was Joan. When either of them listened to me play, we talked a lot more than I played.

Joan was a great source of information and hope for the future. She assured me that life as a sister would get better. She was much more independent as a junior sister than she had been the first two years.

One afternoon Joan came in quietly to study while I practiced. I stopped playing the Beethoven sonata I was working on and turned around to face her.

"I have to ask you about what Sister Beatrice said a few

weeks ago."

Joan sat down, opened her book randomly so it would look like she was studying, and looked up at me. "What did she say?"

"Well, S. Beatrice looked so serious I almost felt sorry for her. And then she started on how important community is and how you have to be friends with everyone. You know, the normal talk. But then she said we had to be careful who we talked to and who we were seen with. I sat there and wondered if somebody had really gotten in trouble--she sounded so serious. Then she said we shouldn't be seen with the same postulant three times in a row. We should try to talk to someone different every day and spend our time equally with all our sisters. We didn't want to have a 'particular friendship' with anyone, and if we were seen together more than three times, people would think we had a 'particular friendship.' "

Joan smiled at me and didn't say anything.

"What?" I looked at her. "What's this particular friendship thing? Beatrice was so intense about it. I don't get it. And she talked about some postulants that were whispering at night behind a statue of Mary! Like it was a crime!"

Joan laughed. "You guys got THE talk. She's talking about being a lesbian. That's what it's about. And none of the older nuns know how to say it, so they talk around and around it. But they're deathly afraid that a close friendship will be a lesbian relationship, and they're not about to let that happen. But they can't say it. You have to figure it out on your own."

I felt my face turn red. It had never occurred to me that Beatrice had meant that. Not that I knew exactly what it meant. And there was really no way I could find out. I was too embarrassed to ask Joan anything else.

I had plenty of friends and was seen with them more than three times and they were just good friends.

I laughed with Joan after my red face faded. I was glad I had discovered the mystery around this 'particular' rule. All of us postulants talked about particular friendships after that instruction period, without really knowing what we were talking about. None of my friends admitted being concerned about the rule, but it was always in our minds. I didn't know anyone who was a lesbian, but now I began to wonder about everyone else, and relationships that had looked wonderful now began to look suspicious.

Right before Christmas, S. Beatrice called me in her office. I walked in slowly. It was an ordinary weekday and nothing unusual had happened. But it was like being called to the principal's office in elementary school. Had I forgotten to clean or work in the laundry? Had someone seen me talking to Joan and Maribeth? I had done so many things wrong, I didn't know which one to worry about.

I stood at attention in front of S. Beatrice's desk.

"I have a rather strange request here, Susan," she said simply.

"Yes, sister?"

"You have been requested by one of our Mankato sisters to meet her parents this afternoon. Why do you suppose she wants you to meet them?" she asked, sounding unsure if she should be angry with me.

I thought fast. "Oh, I know," I said brightly. "It might be Sister Joan. She's heard me play the piano and especially likes this one French piece. My piano teacher told me that Sister Joan had asked about it."

I hoped S.Beatrice wouldn't ask any more questions.

"Well, you may go to meet them. But don't stay long and interrupt their visit. I expect you back here to do your cleaning." She waved her hand at me and I left.

I walked down the first-floor corridor to the guest parlor and met Joan's family and parents. Sister Beatrice probably wondered how I knew her so well, but she never asked and I never told her.

Chapter 15
Suicide

Joan and Maribeth and I would also meet in the library on the ground floor and pull up our chairs together and talk. Joan was the bright exuberant one, whereas Maribeth was quiet and reserved. One day as I was opening the door to the library, Maribeth ran past me crying. I asked Joan what was wrong. She said, "Maribeth has a lot of problems. She's depressed a lot." After that conversation Joan and I talked about helping Maribeth whenever we were by ourselves.

One day Joan left a note asking me to meet her in a practice room. She didn't waste words. "Maribeth tried to commit suicide last night and she's in the hospital. I wanted to tell you before anyone else mentioned it."

"Oh my God! Suicide? What did she do?"

"She took lots of pills. I don't even know where she got them. It's lucky somebody found her and got her to the hospital in time."

"Is she going to be okay?"

"I guess so. I hope so."

"I didn't know she was that upset about anything."

Joan was quiet for a moment. "I know she's been down lately, trying to decide if this is really the life for her. And you know she's been seeing S. Eric for months."

"Yeah, I know." S. Eric was on the faculty and was also a psychologist.

"I thought things were better."

"Yeah, I did too." Joan answered sadly.

I was quiet. These were my closest friends, and yet I had no idea that Maribeth was so depressed. This was the first time in my life I had known someone who tried to kill themselves and I couldn't understand. I couldn't imagine anyone wanting to take their own life. And Maribeth was so young and full of life and possibilities. She didn't have to stay in the convent. She could leave anytime and do anything she wanted.

Joan had to go. "I'll let you know when I find out anything else. Like when she'll be back. I'll leave a note."

68

"Tell her I hope she's okay. Oh, I don't know what to tell her. Just tell her I miss her and hope to see her soon. And let me know if I can do anything."

Joan answered sadly, "I'm not really sure there's anything we can do. If S. Eric can't help her, I don't know how we can. But I'll let you know."

I sat in the practice room after she left, staring out at the sulfur plant and the river beyond it. All the trees were brushed with a green tint, thousands of tiny buds waiting for warm weather.

New life, and soon everything in God's creation would be growing. It hurt to think of Maribeth not sharing that love of life.

For the first time in my life, I felt a huge desire to help someone. Not a vague desire to devote my life to helping people in general, but a wish that I could make a difference in one person's life. And I felt so helpless. I hadn't even been aware of what she was going through.

I realized that although we saw each other almost every day, I was usually practicing, and when we met and talked, Joan and I were the ones who kept the conversation going. Maribeth was quieter and more reserved--and now I realized--more depressed.

I couldn't share my worries and concerns with anyone, but I finally got a cryptic note in with my music. "Home. Let us know when."

I wrote down a few of my practice times and left them in the cubbyhole. The next afternoon we met in the library on the top floor. No one else was in sight, but we whispered anyway. Maribeth said she was feeling okay but didn't want to talk about it. She said she was just confused about her life.

She wanted to hear me play, so they came in later as I practiced. I wanted to do so much more, but all I could do was practice like I always did. In the next month, we gradually returned to our normal routine.

Maribeth seemed a little happier, but exams were coming up for all of us and they would be leaving in a few weeks to do their practice teaching up north.

I learned a lot about helplessness those few months. I wanted so much for my friend, but I couldn't give anything to her.

I could be happy and upbeat about life, but it didn't do any good for someone who was depressed. I couldn't give my love of life to her. I realized that the joy in living has to come from inside ourselves.

There were tears and hugs and goodbyes and then they were gone. I didn't know if I'd ever see them again. I knew Joan would be fine in whatever life she chose. And I couldn't even write them a letter next year from the novitiate. Novices couldn't communicate with anyone except family members by letter for the entire year.

Chapter 16
The Bell Tower

Down the fourth-floor corridor, past the classrooms and the swinging doors, was a tall thin door that led to the bell tower. I knew which door it was because I went with Leanne once to ring the huge Angelus bell. The door opened to a wooden room, covered in dust. The sunlight from the open roof filtered down and the dust swirled in the thick yellow light. The staircase was spiral with wooden bannisters attached to the wall on each side. I could see the bell far above me. From what little I could see, it was very large--I couldn't put my arms around it--and greenish-grey. The heavy rope hung down the middle and onto the dusty floor. There was a thin metal pole right next to the rope that rose to the ceiling far above. I thought at the time how neat it would be to walk all the way up the stairs and explore the bell tower.

In the weeks before Christmas, Sister Beatrice talked to us incessantly about how important it was to go to bed early on Christmas Eve so we could get up for Midnight Mass. We had to be asleep by 7:30, then get up at 10:30 to get ready for Mass. She got more and more agitated as we got closer to Christmas. By December 20, she was about to have a fit. She talked for three instruction periods about getting our sleep and how she didn't want anyone to get sick.

"That happened to a postulant a few years ago," she spoke with a deep sigh like it had been a death from the plague.

"And once there was a postulant who fainted," she whispered.

It didn't matter that most of us had probably gone to Midnight Mass most of our lives and managed to live through the experience. Not to mention late night parties in high school. I had never been to an all-night party--any party, actually. But I had gone to Midnight Mass every year. Like little children, we needed to be put to bed early enough to get a few hours of sleep.

In spite of all of S. Beatrice's warnings I started thinking that Christmas Eve might be a good time to explore the bell tower. I asked Elena Martinez, a postulant from California, if she wanted to go up in the bell tower with me that night.

She said, "Sure," without the slightest hesitation. Elena seemed a very free spirit. Was that typical of Californians?

By 7:30 Christmas Eve it was all quiet and dark in our part of the building since everyone was, if not asleep, at least in the dorms trying to sleep. Elena and I waited about ten minutes after the lights went off and then I peeked out the door to the corridor. No one was there. As we hurried down the long dark corridor, I was rapidly thinking of an excuse for us being awake in case we ran into someone. We slipped through the swinging doors into prohibited territory and walked right up to the bell tower door.

I put my hand on the doorknob, hoping at the last second that it wasn't locked. It creaked open and we slid in and closed the door behind us. We couldn't turn on the light. There was a ghostlike light far above us from outside, but the room was shrouded in darkness. I pulled up my skirts and felt with my big heavy shoe for the first step. The stairway had been made for a size three shoe, so I had to climb on the outer edge of them, on my tiptoes, holding my skirts with my left hand and the metal pole with my right. I didn't want to accidently grab hold of the bell rope. Accidently ringing the bell would have been a tremendously loud announcement to the whole motherhouse that we were trespassing. We climbed slowly in the dark.

My foot didn't quite hit the next step and I stumbled, reaching out blindly. I missed the rope by an inch and grabbed the metal pole instead. It was freezing, but I was sweating. We finally reached the top. The winter night was a faint glow of moonlight and starlight and grey clouds, just a little brighter than the velvet blackness inside the tower. The huge bell was directly above me, and to the side of it I could barely make out a small door which led to the roof.

I heard Elena stumble behind me. I turned to see her on her knees, cursing loudly in Spanish. I pushed open the trapdoor and crawled out on the roof. She stumbled out behind me.

"Don't close the door!" I called quickly and found a brick to hold it open. I could imagine them finding our frozen bodies a few days later on the roof.

Elena suddenly stopped cursing and stood up and twirled in the snow.

72

"This is so beautiful! I've never seen snow falling before. Look at it! It's everywhere. And it's so quiet. Look at my arms."

She held out her arms and I could see the snowflakes on the black serge, then melting just as quickly. Elena kept laughing in delight.

The roof sloped downward on both sides, but there was a ridge along the top where we stood. The sky was dark and full of gray snow clouds. The soft snow drifted down quickly. The roof was already white, and our black capes and skirts captured each snowflake as it fell. We tried to find the prettiest ones. The dim night sky made a gray haze of the snow, and it seemed like twilight.

"Look at this one." I held out my arms and caught as many snowflakes as possible.

"Oh, look. Mine's better. This is the prettiest thing I've ever seen! I never knew falling snow looked like this!"

It was quiet. The clouds muffled any noise from the city. We could see far down to the river on one side, and through the snow we could see some red and green flickering lights of a barge. I could see the lights on many of the houses. They twinkled off and on in the distance until the gray clouds swallowed them.

Everything was silent, muffled by the snow. I imagined the words to "Silent Night" of a century ago. We stood there shivering in the cold and wind and snow, but neither one of us turned to go back inside. We didn't say much, but just watched the world quietly. It finally got so cold that we had to go in. I couldn't feel my nose any longer and I was starting to shiver. I caught a last look at the cold river, with a few barges, and the snow peacefully dancing in the dim light. I knew that I would always remember this first Christmas away from home.

A few years ago, I visited the motherhouse for only the second time in 45 years and asked about Elena. My friend told me she was still a sister and actually lived in the motherhouse. She whispered that Elena had always had a problem with depression. It was an awkward meeting; she seemed not as friendly or happy as she had been so many years ago. I asked her if she remembered the Christmas Eve on the roof. She said no, and the conversation turned to other classmates and other topics.

I felt so bad. The night was so vivid in my mind, such an important memory. I wished she had remembered it. It made me sad that her life had not turned out well. I wished she had seen more of the beauty of the world around her and that she had remembered those moments, that silent night years ago.

Chapter 17
Dear Lord!

I didn't think much of formal prayer. One honest prayer from the heart was better than meaningless repetitions of words that someone else had written.

It didn't take more than a few days in the convent to realize how much we would actually be praying. Even as I woke in the morning, slowly sat up in bed, and looked out the window, the first thing that came into focus, with the help of my ugly convent glasses, was the grey outline of the chapel against the orange and reddish dawn sky.

After the hour-long morning meditation in the chapel, a nun would walk up in front of the pews and start to chant Lauds, the morning prayer. We would all rise and chant with her the beautiful psalms of the Old Testament. After January the postulants would be leading the prayer. I dreaded the day I would have to stand up there and lead the entire congregation. I prayed it wouldn't be for a long time, or maybe I would somehow get missed in the rotation.

Lauds is part of the Divine Office, a centuries old prayer recited and sung by nuns and priests. The Divine Office, also known as the Liturgy of the Hours, was especially important in the monastic orders.

All of the prayers had Latin names. The big ones were Lauds, the early morning prayer,

Vespers at five in the afternoon, and Compline at night. Each prayer lasted about twenty minutes, and consisted mostly of psalms, but with Mass, meditation, the Rosary, listening to readings during meals, and instructions, the prayer time really added up.

I'd gauge the weather for the day by the windows. During our morning prayers the stained-glass windows would turn to vibrant colors as the daylight brightened the world outside. Sometimes in winter, the grey windows would remain dark and colorless, reflecting deep clouds that covered the city, heavy with rain or snow.

After meditation and Lauds, we celebrated Mass. By 1966, the great reforms of the Second Vatican Council had already taken place. The Mass was said in English instead of Latin, and the priest faced the congregation. The church was frantically, and often with great resistance both within and without, trying to make the changes. The Council had made sweeping changes that required quick changes. There was no transition period at all. Gregorian chant was out, to be replaced by hastily written guitar songs in English to fill the vacuum. All the readings and parts of the Mass had to be hastily translated and thrown into use.

Being a liberal Catholic made me want all the changes, but I cringed at the horrible music written quickly and badly, while centuries of great music by Bach and Gregorian Chant were tossed aside only because they were in Latin. Composers appeared from nowhere, some with very little talent, trying to provide the new translations with music that fit. Some of it was good. Most of it was terrible.

After Mass we ate breakfast in silence, listening to stories of saints who would supposedly inspire us, although I never quite understood how. A lot of them were virgins and martyrs, not exactly what I was striving for. I was still a virgin but being a martyr didn't interest me in the least.

Afterwards, all thirty-two of us could walk outside and talk for a while before our instructions began. It was a few moments of freedom. We'd go quickly out the side door to whatever weather greeted us, and then head down the long driveway in front of the motherhouse. The green lawns with their massive oak trees stretched off all the way down to the railroad tracks, and beyond that, to the Mississippi River. We'd walk quickly, talking about what had happened the day before, or what would happen that day, and sometimes we'd walk to the old cemetery down at the end of the driveway. It was surrounded by an iron picket fence, heavily rusted. Even though it was mowed, the weeds came up around the headstones. A few fresh flowers would mark the grave of some sister who had recently died. But we were young and didn't know anyone buried in the cemetery, so we talked all the way down, stopped to say a cursory prayer, and continued around the building, laughing and gossiping all the way. We were a lot more teenagers than nuns.

We'd circle back to kitchen square where we went in an

open door. We would run upstairs, still laughing and talking, to our study hall for instructions. Starting at 8:00 a.m. every morning, S. Beatrice would drone on for an hour. We'd listen to her read the Bible, and stories about saints, but mostly we'd listen to explanations of rules. The hour was always too long, and my mind would drift to a hundred different places. Then we would take our books and go to our morning classes.

I'd walk over to the music department to practice piano for an hour or two each day as part of my music degree. That was a joy. Most of the time I'd have to practice on the upright pianos in the tiny practice rooms, but sometimes I would get to play in the large hall with two wonderful grand pianos. And I spent a lot of time talking to my friends Maribeth and Joan. We talked about rules, their lives, where they had grown up, what their families were like, what life would be for all of us when we graduated and went out on mission. How the church was changing. If the habits would ever change. If the church would become more liberal.

By 3:30 p.m., all our classes were over, but instead of studying or talking, we would gather in the chapel and then walk along the bridge connecting the motherhouse with the college, praying the rosary. When the rosary was finished, we'd have a half of an hour of free time before Vespers. We'd walk silently back to the chapel to pray. At dinner we silently listened to more readings, and then we'd get one hour of recreation. It was often planned for us, with some sport like volleyball or folk dancing. Once a month, we'd get together with the novices or junior sisters for a rushed meet and greet that was over too quickly.

After recreation, we'd come back to the study hall and work on our homework. I'd usually be right in the middle of some assignment when I'd hear the clock chime nine times, and whether we were finished or not, we'd walk to the chapel, pray Compline, and go upstairs to bed.

I wanted to communicate with God, but I couldn't imagine that the stiff words of centuries past were what he or she wanted to hear. We were young and were told to be patient. Someday we would realize the importance of all this prayer. We had to have faith that the prayer was having some kind of miraculous effect on those we prayed for, from someone dying in Africa or China to the homeless on the streets of St. Louis. We were told that our prayers worked whether we could see the result or not. I hoped somebody was being helped, because I certainly didn't see the point.

Chapter 18
The Villa at Christmas

Our first Christmas in the convent was uneventful. In spite of all of S. Beatrice's worries, no one got sick from the late hours on Christmas Eve. Even Elena and I were healthy, despite our adventure on the freezing roof.

We visited with our families the day after Christmas. How strange it was to see them. We were living in two different worlds, and I felt more and more separated from them as I lived this odd, new life. There were only a few hours to talk about all the things that had happened in our lives. I was selfish like many teenagers, and thought I knew enough about their lives, and that mine was the exciting and different one. I tried to explain things about our lives, like how we prayed so much, all the important things I was learning in school, and some of my dreams about the progressive church, but they didn't seem all that interested. Or maybe I just couldn't put into words what my life was really like. And I don't remember paying much attention to theirs. My sisters had children and marriage problems. I had no idea what to say to any of them. And there were so many people. The children, my two sisters, my parents. There wasn't a moment to talk about anything important, not that we would have been able to anyway. I felt unsatisfied and lonely after the visit.

Christmas Eve is the first time that Christmas hymns can be sung in the Catholic liturgy. The weeks preceding Christmas are called Advent, and no Christmas hymns are allowed. This puts us out of sync with the popular culture, which plays Christmas hymns from Thanksgiving till Christmas, then abruptly ends them at midnight on Christmas day.

Because of that rule, all of us postulants went on a bus a few days after Christmas to sing at our order's home for elderly sisters, the Villa. Although I didn't want to go to the Villa, it was still exciting to be on a bus. It felt glorious, even though the day was gray and the sky cloudy and the roads wet and sloshy from melted snow. We were all thrilled to be out of the motherhouse for a little while. That's how desperate we were!

I sat next to Pam. "Hey, how was your visit yesterday? I

asked her.

"It was ok," Pam seemed awfully quiet. "How about yours?"

"Kind of weird, I guess. I mean, I missed them and everything, but I feel so far away from them, like in a whole different world."

Pam nodded. "Yeah, I really miss them. Seeing my sisters and brothers for just a few hours didn't make me feel any better. It made everything worse. I miss being with them at Christmas, all the fun and the presents and the Christmas dinner and my grandma and grandpa and everything." Pam looked like she was going to cry.

I missed my family too, but not like that. We never did much for Christmas anyway, and now that my sisters were gone, it was actually kind of lonely at home at Christmas, just like any other day. I missed the feeling of being comfortable with them. I felt like a stranger with my own family.

I stared at the traffic and stop lights and the department stores with their Christmas decorations. They belonged to another world. I never appreciated how wonderful it all looked. It had been a long four months.

We parked at the Villa, a sad old brick building very much like the motherhouse itself, but much smaller. We walked in and talked to some of the older nuns for a while. I was terrible at knowing what to say, so I kind of hung in the background, hoping we'd be singing soon. We finally walked up on a small stage and sang our carols. Pam and I stood next to each other. When the last note died away, I could hear one of the little old nuns in a wheelchair say in a booming playground voice, "When did they start letting darkies in the order?"

We all just stood speechless as another nun quickly walked up to the old nun and started to wheel her out of the room. The only sound for that whole minute was the squeaky wheelchair as it was rolled down the hall.

The superior of the Villa stood up and walked to the front and smiled.

"Thank you so much for singing today. It's such a thrill for our sisters to have you here. Please have some cookies and hot

80

chocolate before you leave."

I glanced at Pam. Her face was impassive, even though I knew she had heard the nun. It was impossible not to have.

I didn't say anything to Pam that day, but we talked about the old nun's comment a lot in the next few weeks. I was appalled, but Pam seemed to take it in stride--just like she had expected something like that to happen. It certainly hadn't been the first time that Pam had experienced prejudice. Pam shrugged it off. "That little old nun is too old to start thinking in a new way. She comes from generations of whites who treated us as slaves, separated us from our families, and sold us. I'm just glad I'm not going to be out on mission with her!"

The civil rights movement was a strong and powerful force in this country in 1966, but that day at the Villa made me realize what Pam already knew. Equality had a long way to go.

I didn't know at all what Pam knew. Her world and experience were completely different from my middle-class, white world. I knew racism existed and felt it was terrible, but I had never experienced it.

I had experienced discrimination only once--as a woman. The company my father worked for, a steel company, had a four-year scholarship given to an employee's child with the highest SAT scores. It was open to any student who was a senior.

I had the highest score and my parents could certainly use the scholarship money. But a boy who got a much lower grade on the SAT got the scholarship. My father was furious, one of the few times I had ever seen him angry. He went and talked to the management of the company. They explained that the boy had a higher chance of coming back and working for the company, but I, as a woman, would probably never work there. They gave the scholarship to the boy. My father couldn't do a thing about it. That was my experience with discrimination, and it hurt a lot. My dad was completely powerless to fight it.

But that was nothing compared to what Pam and most black people had to experience almost every day.

Chapter 19
Fashion School

One morning after Christmas I woke up with a sore throat. It wasn't so bad that I could stay in bed all day, but it did hurt. I got up and stared at all my clothes. I wanted so much to be home, walking out of my bedroom at home with just my robe on, and hearing my mom say, "Sue, are you alright?" and sit down and relax with a cup of hot chocolate.

Instead I dutifully put all the clothes on again. I was so tired of the ugly habit. When I got to the chapel and began the morning meditation, all I could think about, besides my burning throat, were these hideous clothes. I started daydreaming about fashion, or the lack of it.

I had never been interested in fashion. Our elementary school uniform consisted of a white blouse and a solid blue pleated skirt. My high school required a white blouse and a blue plaid pleated skirt. The skirt had to come down well below the knees, and we also had to wear a velvet piece of material pinned to our collars, color coded for the year. Green for freshman, red for sophomores, blue for juniors, and black for seniors.

Even though we didn't have much interest or money for fashion, my friend Donna and I used to leaf through Seventeen Magazine. Donna was a blonde who wore her hair in the bouffant style like the rest of us. We mostly we just laughed at the wild clothes that Twiggy and her friends wore in London. We also realized that most fashions were too expensive for us.

I never had a job in high school that could have paid for more clothes. My parents wanted me to spend my time studying. I preferred that as well, because I wanted to get a good scholarship to a prestigious college or university.

I rarely went anywhere with my high school friends, so good clothes were never required. After the long bus rides to and from school, no one was interested in going anywhere else. Rosati-Kain was located in central St. Louis and its students came from all over the city and surrounding county. I didn't have any neighborhood friends to hang out with since all my schoolmates were miles away.

82

My social life consisted of talking on the phone in the evening. I would ask Mom or Dad if they wanted to use the phone, and if neither one did, I would pull the one black phone into my bedroom and shut the door. I talked to Donna for hours. Giggling and planning our next wild adventure.

By the time Donna and I were juniors, we would meet downtown every other Saturday to go shopping, but we rarely bought anything. We'd just have fun, smelling perfumes, looking at jewelry, sometimes even trying on clothes. Then we'd have a hamburger, chocolate shake and fries at the Walgreen's counter and giggle about the people we saw. We'd look for cute men that reminded us of our favorite movie stars because high school boys were so immature and stupid. We didn't even think about them. We wouldn't have known what to say if any man or boy had actually talked to us.

Sometimes we'd walk the few blocks down to the riverfront and get on the Admiral. It was an excursion steamboat that made two or three hour-long jaunts up and down the river every day. It had four stories and back in its heyday in the 1930's, held over four thousand people. By the sixties, it had lost its charm and very few people got on board. For teenagers like Donna and me, there were places to get hamburgers and sodas on board and play the pinball machines. We were too cool for the pinball machines. Old drunks clutching their paper bags would sit quietly and stare at the river. We would watch the river too, sipping our cokes and talking about our futures.

I slipped out of my daydream as Mary Anne stood up, walked out of the pew to the front of the chapel to begin Lauds. Our hour of meditation was over and I realized I had spent the whole hour daydreaming about fashion and high school and the river.

Maybe it was a punishment for daydreaming, because when we sat down for our morning instructions, it turned out to be about "fashion." Wearing the habit was horrible, but I found out that morning that wearing the habit wasn't the worst thing in the world. Sister Beatrice walked up to the podium as usual.

"Postulants, as you know, your beautiful habits were made by our excellent seamstresses, Sister Calasanctia and Sister

Anastasia. You should thank them for the work they have done over the years for all the postulant classes. But now, since you are about to become sisters in our order, you will have not only the responsibility, but also the privilege of making your own habits for the next year."

I looked over at Pam on the other side of the room. She had a dazed look on her face.

"You will be learning to sew, not as a class, but as individuals under the guidance of our sewing teachers. They will be helping, but you will be doing the work. In the sewing room are cubbyholes with your names. They contain all the materials you will need. Don't wait too long to get started! The sisters will be there to help you."

I sat paralyzed with fear. I had never even looked at a sewing machine. Some of my friends had taken home economics in high school, but my college prep high school never even offered it. We were all preparing to go to college and studying what we thought were more important things.

I looked down at what I was wearing, not that I hadn't seen it before. But it looked very different when I realized I would be making one just like it. The dress was made of thick black serge, a wool-like material. It had a hem, pleats, buttons and snaps, sleeves and a collar. And I was supposed to learn how to make this in less than six months? I suppose if I had been able to work at it full time, I could possibly have done it, but I still had to go to school, practice the piano, and pray most of the day. When would I have the time? When would any of us have the time?

The sewing room was conveniently located right outside our study hall. I had never even set foot in it, avoiding it like you cross the street to avoid the gossiping neighbor. It had long rows of sewing machines and there were two wizened nuns who seemed to always be there. I always felt sorry for them because of their names. Who would have ever chosen Calasanctia or Anastasia for their lifelong names?

I suppose if I had been smart, I would have figured out that there was a reason for the long rows of sewing machines, and long tables in the middle of the room. But it had never occurred to me that I would be in that room at all.

If there is a God, I hope he has a very special place for our two sewing teachers. And yes, I do mean heaven instead of hell. I had to be their worst pupil in many years. I needed to learn how to operate the machine and the foot pedal and thread the thing and get the tension just right. And that was only the beginning. Measuring, cutting the material just right, sewing hems, taking them out because they weren't perfect, and then redoing them. I'd drag myself into the sewing room almost every afternoon for my daily dose of humiliation and frustration, and the only vow I made that year was to never sew anything else in my entire life. The collar had to be redone three times. My buttonholes were the size of the Grand Canyon and the buttons themselves tried their hardest to hang on and not come undone. The pleats on the skirt had no idea which direction they were headed.

But the two nuns were patient. They didn't have anything else to do. If I had been rich, I would have paid them to sew the stupid dress for me. But finally, at the end of June, all of our habits were made for the following year--except for Juliette. Hers was made so poorly that it was unwearable and the two sewing sisters ripped it apart and redid it for her. I wasn't so lucky with mine. I had to wear it.

I remember standing in the sewing room with my new habit on, feeling not the slightest bit of accomplishment. Looking at this heavy black serge dress that sucked every ounce of femininity out of me, how could I feel anything? My only feeling was relief that it was over. And I made my own special vow that I would never sew anything like that again. That was one vow I kept.

Chapter 20
Sister Beatrice's Bad Day

When Sister Beatrice felt strongly about something, we postulants would hear about it for weeks, like threads woven through every instruction period. She'd even pick up the thread at the lunch reading and at dinner. Most of the time the readings were innocuous but often I think she lay awake at night poring over the book and choosing paragraphs that got her points across. Subtlety wasn't Sister Beatrice's strength.

During instructions, Sister Beatrice tried to teach us about the Bible. She had run out of rules to explain after a few months and we went on to the Bible itself. We were reading the passage about how Jesus appeared to the disciples after his resurrection, on the road to Emmaus. It isn't a bad reading; it tells a lot about Jesus and about the thinking of his disciples. But Sister Beatrice was like a drug addict, overdosed on "the road to Emmaus." We read and re-read the passage each day in instructions, and Sister Beatrice talked incessantly about it. I remember waiting for her to provide some incredible insight into the reading, but she never did. We just sat day after day and listened. We were on the road to Emmaus for a month, much longer than Jesus had been there.

One morning Sister Beatrice walked into the study hall quickly, her face set like stone.

We were waiting not so quietly for our "road to Emmaus marathon," but with one look at her face, we became very quiet.

"Martha, close the door."

When the doors were closed, that meant either some notable religious figure had died, a classmate had left the convent, or we were in big trouble. I glanced around the room. Nobody seemed to be missing, although traces of the defectors were wiped out so quickly, sometimes we didn't even notice they were gone.

"Postulants," her voice was low and tortured. "I can hardly bring this matter up, but I feel I have to. Sister Philippa was checking for some clothes yesterday up in YOUR dorms, and she…found…this!"

Sister Beatrice's face was red now, and puffy. She looked like a balloon about ready to explode. She held up an

86

unrecognizable paper bag, her voice squeezed out low and hard.

"Brownies…in…the…UNDERWEAR!"

Then softer, "Brownies…in…the…underwear."

Then a pained whisper, "Brownies…in…the…underwear."

She stopped to let the horror of it sink slowly into our minds. I madly tried to figure out what she was talking about. I stole a glance at Pam, but she didn't know either. She was trying to stifle a giggle.

Sister Beatrice continued with great difficulty.

"Yes, postulants, a member of your class received these brownies on visiting day, and instead of sharing them with her sisters, she," her voice sank lower and lower," hid them…in her…drawer."

Her voice had sunk to its lowest. She could no longer continue. She stopped a moment to regain control.

"Postulants, this is not the first time something like this has happened, and it will not be tolerated anymore!" She ended on a scream that practically rattled the windows. If anything could be said, Sister Beatrice certainly had a flair for the dramatic. I realized that she had missed her calling. She was a born actress.

She got out her white handkerchief and wiped her red face, which was slowly returning to its normal shade of pink. She folded the handkerchief neatly and placed it in her pocket.

With an audible sigh, she managed to intone, "That is all, postulants."

She then stepped down from the podium and walked into her office.

All of us sat perfectly still, hardly daring to breathe. We couldn't move. Were there going to be any more instructions? Someone in the front row coughed. Then silence again. How could anyone get up and leave the study hall? They would have walk by the front door of S. Beatrice's office, which was still open. How frightening to just get up and leave. What if she were coming back out to continue instructions after she recovered from the shock of the brownies?

We sat. Joan sneezed and looked very guilty about it. I stole another glance at Pam. She shrugged her shoulders slightly. Pam couldn't get up, though I knew she was itching to get out of there. Pam didn't like being anywhere near trouble since she had the bad fortune of always getting caught right in the middle of it.

We sat. I watched the second hand go around on the wall clock. It was only eleven minutes past eight and our instructions usually went on till nine. I wondered if I could get out a book and start reading. But my desk top squeaked and I knew it would make too much noise. Maybe Ruth would leave. Ruth was Beatrice's favorite. She was smart, beautiful, a natural leader, and always abided by the rules. She never got in trouble. She could leave first.

Just then, Sister Philippa opened the study hall doors. She glared at us. Her voice shattered the silence.

"Don't you have any DUTIES, postulants? Are you going to sit there all day sulking?"

We panicked. Books fell. Papers fluttered. Drawers opened and shut. It was more effective than any fire drill. All of us were out of the room and down the corridor in less than sixty seconds, looking desperately for something, anything, to do.

The brownies knocked us all down to that horrible postulant's level. We found out right after instructions that it was Laura who had stuffed the brownies in her drawer, but all of us suffered for it. Sister Beatrice looked at all of us with great suspicion for at least a month afterwards. If Laura could commit this heinous act, then each one of us could do something as bad or worse.

We heard about the brownies in the underwear so much that I wished we could go back to talking about Jesus on the road to Emmaus. After a few weeks the whole incident began to be forgotten, but it was a long time before Sister Beatrice smiled again.

Chapter 21
Music

Even though I was beginning to lose faith in the order and the reforms of the Church, I could at least take refuge in my music.

In high school, after Donna and I would get off the Admiral in downtown St. Louis, I would sometimes drag her to the Steinway store where I'd stare in the window longingly at the pianos.

"Just for a few minutes," I promised.

She reluctantly agreed, as long as we didn't stay too long.

We walked in the door, setting off a tinkling bell, and I brushed my hand along the smooth mahogany wood of the pianos in the showroom. They were all beautiful. I didn't care for fashion, but I cared a lot about pianos.

The salesman looked up and over his thick black-rimmed glasses. He had seen us before, and although Donna and I were obviously high school students, he knew I could play and probably figured we were harmless. He didn't bother to get up. We wouldn't be buying a piano, but we certainly couldn't steal one either.

We took the elevator to the fifth floor where all the grand pianos lived. I was like a kid in a candy store. I tried one, then another and another. This one was great for Bach. It had a nice crisp touch. The one over by the corner was better for Chopin, its bass clear and not muddy. It was a joy to play these instruments, even for a few minutes.

Donna would listen politely, then finally clear her throat. It was time to go home, and we had to catch the Lindell bus before it got dark. Plus, she was bored.

I had a piano at home, a small upright that I played every day. On the wall behind the piano was a gold starburst clock, right out of the fifties, which was when Mom and Dad purchased it. I started taking lessons when I was five years old, like most everyone else. The piano was an integral part of the middle-class home, and back in the fifties piano lessons were practically mandatory. My sisters both took lessons, but neither of them took to it like I did.

I started lessons from a grey-haired old lady named Mrs. Sale. Actually, I have no idea how old she was. I was only five, and every adult seemed old. I did fine for a few weeks, but then I had to learn an F# in a piece called "A frog he would a wooing go." I was brought to tears. I just didn't understand sharps at all. After a week of crying about it, Mom wisely let me quit, but I couldn't stay away from the piano and a year later I started lessons again. This time it took. I loved playing. I could sight read quickly, better than I could read letters, and soon I was going through piano books as quickly as possible.

A pianist named Van Cliburn won the Tschaikovsky Competition in Moscow in 1958. My sister Carol and I wore out his award-winning recording--playing it over and over again on our large maple stereo cabinet in the living room--and he was so cute! My dad would play his own records too. He was a tenor and loved to listen to Caruso and John McCormick and the great tenors of the time. Our home was always full of music.

I never played a grand piano until I was in high school, but I played for a choir festival and got to play one on stage. I was hooked on the sound and dreamed of owning one someday. At least I could play the ones in the Steinway store for a few minutes!

My musical taste was different than anyone else I knew. My favorite composer was Bach. I fell in love with Glenn Gould's recordings of Bach--and he was cute too. Well, not cute, but handsome in a brooding and eccentric way. Forget movie stars. I was in love with pianists. When the Beatles appeared on the Ed Sullivan show I grudgingly watched the show while reading a textbook, but I couldn't see what the big deal was. I hated Elvis Presley and his music. King of what? I was a real musical snob. If they had baseball-type cards for young male pianists, I would have collected them all!

By the time I got to the convent, I knew I had to major in music. And since I couldn't decide which subject I loved more, I majored in English too. Hopefully, if a school didn't need teachers in one subject, they might in another. I got to practice every day. Practicing became a real source of freedom in my otherwise regimented life.

I could give up wearing nice clothes; I could give up sex

because I didn't even know what I was giving up; I could give up my freedom to make decisions--well, some of them; I could give up material possessions because I didn't have any. But I could never give up my music.

Chapter 22
Two Windows

Without my two windows, one at the head of my bed and the other at my side, I might have left the convent that first year. There were only three of us in my small dorm. I don't remember who slept next to me or who was in the third bed--we weren't permitted to speak to each other in the dorm.

I don't remember ever speaking to them once that entire year. Maybe I talked to them downstairs, but there were never whispers or giggling when the lights were out. Never a quick gossip about what had happened during the day or what might happen in the morning. Not even what time it was during the middle of the night. Just nothing. There was complete silence. I find it odd that I lived with these people for eight hours every night and have no idea what they looked like or even who they were to this day.

My friends were my windows.

The single light on our ceiling was turned off at exactly nine-thirty every night, but sometimes instead of lying down I would sit on my bed cross-legged and look out to the world beyond. The window at the side of my bed looked down to Kitchen Square and across to the chapel. The big kitchen bordered the square, but at night it was silent and closed. A few lights might be on in the upper floors, perhaps someone working late in their office or classroom, but all the lights would be out by eleven. Even the stained glass of the chapel windows was dark.

I'd lay on my stomach with my hands holding up my chin and look out the window at the head of my bed. Past the dark road below and the green lawns stretching far in the distance, I could see the trees and rooftops of the small houses, lit only by moonlight, that made up the small, poor city of Lemay.

The brick houses were unbelievably small, even smaller than the tiny house I had grown up in. They were mostly hidden by large oak trees, but I could see their lights twinkling at night and wondered about the people who lived in them.

In the summer I slept with both windows open wide. They were old casement windows and I had to unlock their white latches and push hard on the brittle chipped wood to get them to go up. Getting them to stay up was sometimes a challenge. I used a ruler or a book to prop them open. The humid hot air hung outside without a breeze. Crickets and sometimes cicadas chirped in the sultry night.

I'd wake to the sound of thunder and then hear the welcome drops of rain, cooling down the night for a few hours until sunrise. Sometimes the sheet lightning would light up the whole sky like a sequence of camera flashes. Each flash would turn the whole square inside the window frame into a sudden gray picture, its image frozen in my mind like an old black and white photograph before it faded away in the darkness.

There was an electric light high on the corner of the building across the square. It lit up all of Kitchen Square and cast its dark shadows across the second and third floor porches and dark overhangs.

Sometimes the rain pushed in huge sheets of water across the square. Wave after wave of blowing rain beat up against the brick building. In winter I'd take my hand and wipe the frost off the window to see the first flurries of snow in the light. Sitting entranced, I'd pray for the snow to continue and watch it for hours into the night; its quiet softness silently but steadily spinning a web of white over the concrete square and the roof far above.

When I'd look out my other window, the city and its twinkling lights would be lost in the swirling snow. The frost would etch delicate lines across each pane. After a while, I'd lie down to sleep with the warm blankets wrapped tightly around me.

Sometimes the wind came in through the crack in my window, and I'd wake up freezing, but gradually winter turned into spring and soon the wind brought the softness of warm spring rain. Those were the best nights, when the sound of rain lulled me to sleep, when all creation was green and the warm soft wind would blow the raindrops under the eaves and through the screen to my windowsill.

No matter how many stupid rules or long lectures or endless hours of prayer there were during the day, I knew I could go upstairs at night to my windows.

Our small cubicles had only a bed and a dresser. The bed

had a thin mattress and a plain white bedspread. We learned how to make the beds perfectly, the edges neatly folded and tucked under the mattress. For some reason that was very important. There were no pictures on the wall, just plain white walls. I had nothing on top of my dresser, no pictures of family or friends, no treasures from my previous life. My treasures were outside the windows; the wind, the rain, the snow, and the stars in the night sky.

Chapter 23
My Home Visit

I hadn't been home since I'd joined almost a year before. I saw my parents and my sister Carol who came to see my every month, but once I went into the novitiate, I wouldn't be able to see my family for a whole year. Because of that rule we were given a chance to visit our homes for a week before we entered the novitiate.

As I got out of my parent's car and started up the sidewalk, the house looked so tiny. I couldn't believe I had ever lived there. When I walked inside, everything was the same, including my room. My old desk, radio and bed were still in my room. My parents hadn't gotten around to changing anything; I knew they still hoped I'd be back.

The first day I was home, relaxing as best I could in my habit--it wasn't like we got to dress in shorts and a blouse--my parents received a disturbing phone call. My sister Jane in New York found out her husband Tom was having an affair with his secretary. He showed no remorse, and she took her three children, one an infant, and left him. It came as a complete shock to all of us. In 1967 the divorce rates weren't as high as they are now, and divorce was still considered a terrible tragedy. And it was even worse in the eyes of the Catholic Church.

Many years later my sister told me that she had gone to see her parish priest about Tom's affair. The priest said, "You can't get a divorce. You have to work things out with him." And then he said, "What you really need to do is go home and pray about this." Jane walked out of the office and never again set foot in a Catholic church.

The divorce was horrible for my sister. My parents helped her financially and emotionally. I didn't know what to think about the divorce. Tom had seemed nice enough, very concerned about money and prestige and getting ahead, but I had no idea what their lives were really like. I completely agreed that she should divorce him. I didn't care what the Catholic Church thought about her decision. She would have to raise her children by herself without anyone to help, and I felt awful for her.

My home visit rightfully got shoved to the background in the light of those events, but it did make me realize how little I wanted a traditional marriage and children in my future. Marriage just seemed messy, and not worth all the trouble it brought. I had no interest in having children, and the only man I had ever been interested in was just a high school crush on an older teacher. And I was smart enough to realize that's what it was.

My sister Jane was married to a man who cheated on her. My sister Carol had married Jerry, a guy she met in a bar. He had a boat that he would take out on the river, and he asked her to marry him. None of us thought very much of him. I was going through my snob phase, one I never really grew out of, and when I found out he didn't appreciate classical music and Shakespeare, wrote him off as a bad choice. He cheated on her too, so he did end up being a bad choice.

All the boys I knew in high school, which weren't many, were so immature I couldn't even imagine talking to them. It wasn't that I didn't like men, I just didn't know any real men, other than my father and grandfather. They were wonderful, but they were my relatives- a completely different category.

When we got back to the motherhouse, each one of us had an interview with Sister Alphonse, the mother superior of the whole convent. She didn't know any of us but would be making the final decision about our vocations. She asked me a few questions about my studies and my faith, and then asked me a question about my friendships with older sisters in the community.

That question took me off guard, because Joan, Maribeth and I had been very careful about hiding our friendship. I would have been in so much trouble if S. Beatrice knew that I talked to them every day, much more often than I talked to members of my class. And I never had gotten in trouble for it, so I didn't understand how the mother superior even knew. I guess I came up with a pretty good excuse, telling her that I had two older sisters and was better at relating to older women than my contemporaries. More than that I didn't dare say.

I passed the interview just like everyone else and got ready to enter the novitiate.

Chapter 24
Are You Happy?

We had our last visiting day the Sunday before we entered the novitiate. I came out on the front lawn, pleased that everyone had come to visit. Jane had just moved back from New York and my sister Carol came with her two children. We tried to talk and catch up with all the news, but I was in my own world in every way possible, from the closed-in walls of the building to my distance from the day-to-day family affairs.

I felt hot and uncomfortable with our awkward conversation. Jane was going through a divorce, Carol was working and raising her two children, my dad was still working at a steel factory, and my mother had just started teaching in the St. Louis public schools.

I had put up a wall between us, and I was painfully aware of just how high and thick it had become, like the walls of the motherhouse itself. I couldn't tell them what my life was really like. They would have insisted that I leave immediately--and I found it difficult to catch up or even be interested in theirs.

As usual, my dad asked if I was happy. And as usual, I told him that I was. That was the extent of our conversations, even before I had entered the convent. He never knew quite what to say to any of his girls. He could talk for hours about tennis and politics but seemed at a loss to make conversation about anything else.

S. Alphonse, the mother superior of our province, was out on the lawn for our last visiting day, slowly winding her way through the knots of people scattered across the grass. I alerted the family that she was the mother superior of the whole province, all the way to California, trying to explain that she was like the CEO of a company, and suddenly she was there in our small group.

She inquired how we were all doing. My father got up to shake hands with her and without a moment's hesitation asked, "Are you happy, sister?"

I practically melted with embarrassment at my father's horribly inappropriate question. It was one thing to ask me if I was happy, but to ask anyone else--and someone so important--was just rude.

I took a deep breath, not knowing what to say or do to get both of them out of this awkward situation.

S. Alphonse was very quiet as I cringed. Then she smiled, opened her mouth and said, "Yes, I guess I am happy. I never really thought about it before."

She and my father talked a little more about what he did, what I was doing, she said a few things about her job as superior, and she seemed reluctant to leave. She shook my father's hand and said how good it had been to meet him. I wondered if anyone had ever dared to ask her that question as I breathed a huge sigh of relief.

I always wondered why my dad had asked that question. We never talked much, and talking to my sisters later in my life, realized they had never really talked to him either. I think the question "are you happy?" was a simple and direct way of covering the basics without having to deal with any more complex issues.

I learned quickly that "Yes, I'm happy," was the correct answer, the one he wanted to hear. It's a good thing that I was most often very happy, although I would never have shared my unhappiness.

The bell rang and I hugged everyone, grateful to be going inside. There were a few tears shed, but I was already gone from their lives.

In most Catholic families of the 60's it was a privilege to have a child become a priest or nun. Not in my family. I can't imagine I could have picked a way of life that went so much against my parent's wishes.

My parents were not the typical Catholic family. My dad had emigrated from Hamburg, Germany, in 1927. He was lucky he got out of Germany before Hitler came to power. A few years later it would have been difficult and then impossible to leave the country. His religious tradition was Lutheran, but he never talked about going to church and certainly never went since he was a child.

My dad had one criteria for judging others--whether they could play tennis. He was consumed by the sport. He played with his Christian friends on Saturday, and his Jewish friends on

98

Sunday. He played with a young black high school student, Arthur Ashe, before he grew up to become a famous tennis player. My dad was invited many times to join the exclusive country clubs, but he always played on the free courts at Forest Park because the country clubs wouldn't accept blacks. My dad was color blind. He didn't care where the person was from, what color their skin was, or what language they spoke. All he cared about was whether they could play a good game of tennis.

I think my father was a happy man. He loved his family, and his tennis games and his friends and didn't expect much more out of life. He had everything he wanted.

I wanted more, although I wasn't sure what I wanted. Going into the novitiate, I thought I was on the right track. I had a lot of what I wanted to be happy. I was going to school getting a good college education. I was becoming a sister--something I had chosen and still hoped would be a good way of life. I loved God deeply and my desire to serve God surpassed all the petty rules and regulations we had been subjected to. I held onto my belief that God had a plan for me and I was in the process of discovering it, along with and very often in spite of the rules.

I had friends. Even though Joan and Maribeth were gone, I had Pam and Juliette and a few other classmates--just enough to be happy. I was not popular in high school. It was the same in the convent. One or two good friends were all I needed to keep going.

I had my music, and a teacher, S. Verene, who was proud of the way I played. I enjoyed learning from her. I wasn't lying when I told my father I was happy because I was.

Chapter 25
The Novitiate

My decision had been made. One muggy afternoon in August, we had a simple ceremony in our Big Chapel and with a few words uttered by the priest, became novices. Everything I had gotten used to in the past year was gone. I had put on my new handmade habit that morning, thanking God that it didn't fall apart instantly, and wore a tighter white veil that covered my hair completely. It looked like a white box on my head, to be honest. We were still waiting for the ugly habit to change. It would happen soon, we were assured.

My classmates and I moved into the middle section of the motherhouse. This was the forbidden section of the building reserved for "real" nuns. We had a whole new section to explore, but our freedom was in name only, since we were only allowed to be in the novitiate and were no longer allowed to go back to the postulant wing.

I missed my windows so much. I was in a large dormitory-- in the center, far away from the windows--and I would dread going upstairs to the dorm and pulling shut the tan curtains with their metal rings. They surrounded my bed on all four sides. We didn't have our own lamps so when the high fluorescent dorm lights went off, our cells were dull and black. When it rained, I never hear the soothing sounds. When it snowed, I couldn't watch the flakes float down past my window. I had to wait until morning to see anything outside. I hated it.

We got a lot of exercise during the day, walking the length of the motherhouse back and forth to classes and prayers, climbing the stairs at least a dozen times a day, so I fell asleep easily and slept well. I still missed my windows. Often when it rained or snowed, I would go to the chapel late at night and watch the snow through a high window in the choir loft. It wasn't enough, but it was all I had.

That first evening we ate in the new dining room. It looked similar to the old one, long tables with a desk at the end where S. Regina introduced herself and then immediately started reading about the saint of the day from that never-ending book, "The Lives of the Saints." Afterwards we went up to our new study hall, which looked just like our old one, only plopped down in a different section of the building.

S. Regina was all business. She didn't crack a smile. She looked out over us and started speaking. "Sisters." Then louder, "Sisters! My name is S. Regina, your novice mistress. I am here to guide you through the next year, and at the end of it, you will become full-fledged sisters in our order. This is not an easy year. You will be tested over and over again to make sure only the best and most worthy of you will go on to represent our order in the world."

She made me feel like a lump of clay, waiting to be formed into something completely different by her. I had no past, no accomplishments, and no dreams. I was just a formless shape waiting to be poured into a mold.

Her face--and I'm being uncharitable--was ugly, like badly arranged putty. It had folds and creases in all the wrong places. She wore a permanent frown--no smile lines anywhere. I realize now that she was probably in her early fifties, but she looked ancient to me. Sister Beatrice, in contrast, had a fleshy red face, but she could smile, and she could be fooled and sometimes manipulated. S. Regina had no soft underbelly. She was completely in charge.

She told us one other thing that evening. "The rule of silence is even more important in this holy year, and it will be observed not only at night, but all day, except for your walks around the motherhouse in the morning and during your hour of recreation. The rest of the time you will be praying and contemplating your future life, not talking. That rule will begin tonight. Good night."

We quietly got up and made our way upstairs.

We didn't have a separate chapel any longer but did all our extensive praying with the other nuns in the Big Chapel. I knew all the splinters and knots of wood in the four wooden pews assigned to us by the end of the year. We learned about theology and even more "rules" in the novitiate. Who knew there could be so many? We had one theology class in the college, and I was lucky enough to still be able to practice every day in the music department. I didn't have the luxury of talking to anyone like I had the previous year, so I just practiced the piano a lot.

But another thing I learned was about relationships. Friendships our first year were tempered with our studies, our prayers, and the newness of our religious life. That fear that S. Beatrice had tried to instill in us about "particular friendships" became even more obvious in the novitiate, when we became completely insulated in our own world, not able to speak to anyone outside of our little group--or even in our little group.

One day had been unexpectedly busy, and after dinner I asked S. Regina if I could practice piano over in the college, even though it was late. She reluctantly said yes but told me I'd have to bring someone with me. The fear of men was everywhere!

I asked another novice named Kate and she grabbed some homework and a philosophy textbook and came with me. She was an acquaintance at best, a little moody but loved philosophy. The sky was dark and rain beat loudly on the windows. I practiced for about an hour in one of the large studios, and then Kate put down her book and came and sat next to me on the piano bench. I was showing her some of my music--she had played the piano when she was younger--when the door opened behind us.

A middle-aged nun, one of the science teachers, looked at us sitting together. She must have seen the light on.

"What are you doing?" she yelled.

Kate jumped up quickly. "We're just talking."

"You shouldn't be in here alone! Get out! And don't let me see you two together again--ever!"

She waited impatiently at the door to make sure we were leaving. I gathered up my music and walked out quickly behind Kate. Neither of us said a word all the way back to the novitiate. Kate and I never talked about the incident. I worried that the teacher might say something to S. Regina. I wondered if I should find the teacher and tell her that nothing had happened--I wasn't even sure what could have happened--but coward that I was, I was afraid to bring it up.

After a year in the convent, I had never seen any evidence of those horrible "particular friendships." I wasn't sure what lesbians "did" that was so terrible. Love was love, but certainly not in the eyes of the church. I was sure there had been instances of

102

"unnatural relationships" between girls. There had to have been, or the superiors wouldn't have been so frightened of it.

Friendship was a scary tightrope that stretched over our group. One wrong step in any direction was dangerous.

One of our stated goals was to make our group a community of women who loved and cared for each other. That was the reason we weren't supposed to talk with anyone else in the motherhouse. We were working hard to make our own little community. But trying to love and care for each other was actively discouraged and frowned upon. And the added problem was that we had very little time to interact with each other. Even that was discouraged. Our recreations at night were filled with volleyball, folk dancing and activities that gave us little time to talk.

Even though those horrible old-fashioned ideas about "particular friendships" were in our minds at all times, the convent was still an endless source of friends. It was like an ice-cream store for extroverts like me. A lot of the flavors were banned, but that just made them even more desirable.

By the end of my first year I had very few friends in my class. Pam was a friend and I loved Juliette--in a friendly way! She turned out to be a caring and compassionate person. But I hardly had time to talk to anyone else.

Maribeth and Joan had been the perfect friends. We could meet and talk in secret. They didn't care what rules they were breaking and neither did I. They had been my best friends, but now that they had gone back to Minnesota I couldn't write to them and didn't know if I'd ever see them again.

Most attempts at friendship were taken underground and built in secret. Not a very good thing if the one thing the authorities are afraid of is secret and unnatural relationships.

We were eighteen and nineteen years old. Years where we should be expanding our world, meeting new people, women and men, learning, gaining new experiences, becoming ourselves. But we had been turned in on ourselves, forgetting who we were, striving to pour ourselves into a mold made hundreds of years ago in a different world.

And all of us got called into the office because of one infraction or another concerning friendship. No wonder we were emotionally stunted. We acted like we had in grade school, with the teacher ready to accuse us of not being nice, of being mean to someone outside the group. We were forced to love everybody without really loving anybody.

I tried to conform to the rules, but my heart wasn't in it. I kept looking ahead to the day when I could be myself, and no one else. It looked like I would have to wait another year at least.

Chapter 26
A Dream

One night a few months after I went into the novitiate I had the strangest dream about my two friends. I was standing in the basement corridor outside our dining room and Joan and Maribeth walked up to me. They both hugged me and Joan slipped a note into my hand as she quickly hurried away. I couldn't be seen talking to them. I looked at the note and it said, "Tonight 10:00 p.m.--empty dorm--fourth floor."

So that night in my dream I walked up to the dorm and they were there with some cokes and snacks and we talked for hours.

I woke up suddenly. What a great dream. It was one of those dreams that felt real, right down to the cokes and the note and the cookies.

In fact, it felt so real that I bored Juliette all the way around the motherhouse on our morning walk by telling her every detail. It had been so real. She was patient, listened and commented kindly that I must be missing them a lot. I agreed.

We sat through instructions and then went our separate ways to do chores. I was cleaning two of the parlors on the main floor just inside the novitiate when I saw Juliette walk up to me quickly. She was always pale, but she looked like she had seen a ghost.

"Sue, they were in the downstairs corridor! I saw them!"

"Who?"

"Joan and Maribeth! They told me to tell you to meet them tonight in the empty dorm."

"No they didn't. What are you talking about?" I laughed, a little annoyed that she would make fun of me like that.

"I'm serious. I'm not kidding. I just saw them and they told me exactly what you told me in your dream."

She looked so serious. And Juliette would never get me into trouble--or lie about anything.

"Yeah, sure." It was one thing to say it at all. But to keep saying it was just mean.

I was expecting her to laugh and say, "Of course not!"

But she didn't. She said, "Ask Joanne and Martha. They saw them too. They were with me. Ask them!"

Martha came up behind Juliette. "Did you know that S. Maribeth and S. Joan are here from Mankato?"

I knew that all three of them couldn't be lying. Juliette wouldn't have had the time to arrange the lie. All I could think about all day was the dream--and the reality. What was happening? Nothing like that had ever happened to me before. I wouldn't have believed it myself except that I had told Juliette BEFORE I saw them.

That night I slipped out of my large dorm, supposedly visiting the rest room, but I climbed silently up the stairs to the large empty dorm. Joan and Maribeth were both there, waiting for me.

We sat on the floor, ate cookies and drank cokes and talked for hours. Maribeth was much better and had come down for one last time to see S. Eric, her psychologist. Joan took the opportunity to come with her for the weekend. They were driving back the next day with another Mankato sister.

It was so wonderful to see them. They knew I couldn't write, but we promised to stay in touch--somehow. They couldn't believe my strange dream, but we had so many other things to talk about that the dream was quickly forgotten. We tearfully said goodbye. I slipped back into the dorm about three am, praying that S. Regina wasn't patrolling the halls, hoping to get a few hours of sleep before the 5 o'clock bell. I thought long and hard about the dream and its eerie precision in foretelling the day's events. It remains one of the strangest things that has ever happened to me, and after all these years, I'm no closer to an explanation than I was when it happened.

Many years later, at least forty years, I was back in St. Louis and I went back to the motherhouse. I knew that Joan and Maribeth had both left the order and gone their separate ways, but I never knew anything else about them. I met an old teacher and we talked about mutual friends. I remembered that she had taught Joan and Maribeth, so I asked her if she knew what had happened to them. I had always wondered about Maribeth because of her suicide attempt and if she had managed to have a happy life. I was sure Joan was happy in whatever life she had chosen.

My teacher looked oddly at me, "Well, Maribeth left the order and got married, and I really don't know where she's living now. But Joan..." She looked at me hesitantly. "I guess nobody told you."

I shook my head. "Told me what?"

"Well, Joan got married and was flying back from Tahiti on her honeymoon. The plane crashed on takeoff and everyone on the airplane died. I'm sorry, I thought you knew."

I walked away filled with an aching sadness. I hadn't ever talked to Joan after that night in the dorms, but I could still see her bright, excited face that day we met, so full of life. I remembered our talks in the practice rooms, how I would play a piece or two and then we would spend the rest of the time talking quietly about rules and how life would get better and what it was like being from Minnesota on a farm, and her parents and mine. So many delightful hours together. I remember meeting her parents, farmers from outside Mankato, so proud of their oldest daughter.

I had lost track of them, but I hoped in my heart they were both happy. I wondered a few times if I could ever get hold of them, but it seemed an impossible task.

It's one thing to have lost track of a friend, and to hope that they would be happy in their lives, but to know that their life was cruelly and tragically cut off just as it was beginning, was heartbreaking. They both had been so important in my life, and yet gone from it forever.

Chapter 27
Juliette and the Bell

Juliette saw her parents often on our walks around the building. Her mother would sometimes stand across the street, looking anxiously to see if she could spot her daughter in the group. Juliette cried a lot less now, at least that I knew about, and I didn't think she was homesick anymore. But as difficult a time as Juliette had as a postulant, it was nothing compared with her being a novice.

S. Regina ruled with an iron hand. She was everywhere, patrolling halls and the study hall with a penetrating eagle eye. Nothing, and I mean nothing, got past her.

I tried to like S. Regina, but she had a perpetual scowl on her face. Keeping us in line was a full-time job. She was everywhere. God is supposed to be omnipresent, everywhere at all times, and S. Regina tried hard to be His replacement. She was as hard as granite. It was difficult to believe that Christianity was the religion of love and joy when dealing with S. Regina.

Even though we had a year of study, silence and meditation, we still had assigned chores, just like our first year. Juliette got one of the most difficult chores--bell duty. She had to wake up at 4:30, a half hour before the rest of us, get dressed, and silently go to the end of the corridor next to the Big Chapel. She rang the large hand bell at 5:00 to wake up much of the convent. There must have been other sisters in the depths of the motherhouse that had their own alarm clocks, but the central portion was awakened by Juliette.

One night Juliette didn't sleep very well. We had a series of thunderstorms roll through the city that night, and she woke up suddenly. She squinted at her alarm clock without putting on her glasses.

"Oh my God, it's 5:00 already!" Her alarm hadn't gone off and she was late. She should have been ringing the bell right at that very moment. She couldn't get in any more trouble or she'd get kicked out.

Trouble in the convent wasn't at all like trouble in the real world. Juliette would fall asleep during morning meditation. Or she'd be talking when she wasn't supposed to. Her shoes would come untied. She didn't bow correctly during prayers. And she never ironed her dress. All sorts of little stuff like that. She just seemed to attract trouble wherever she went.

She jumped out of bed and threw on her bra, t-shirt, black stockings, slip, long woolen dress and cape, the little white cap and then the veil over that.

She put on her black shoes without tying them, felt for her glasses, and tiptoed out of the large dorm as quietly as she could. Then she picked up her skirts and ran down the corridor to where it met the main corridor.

Juliette grabbed the bell and raised it high over her head and suddenly heard the chime of the grandfather clock directly behind her, just one chime. Then it stopped. She turned slightly, waiting for the other four chimes, glanced at the clock, and in the second before she brought the bell down she blinked and looked again. It was 12:30 am, just past midnight. It wasn't 5:00 at all. It was still the middle of the night.

Holding her breath, Juliette brought the bell down slowly with one small escaping "Ting" and muffled it in her heavy skirts.

She stood there holding the bell tightly, wrapped in her serge skirts, wondering if anyone had heard the tiny sound. She looked again at the huge grandfather clock with its gold metallic sun and moon on the faceplate and the words "Tempus Fugit. Her one hand gripped the bell tightly and with the other she wiped the sweat from her forehead. It was 12:31 now. Her alarm clock had really said 12:25 and Juliette mistakenly thought it was 5:00 am. She got the hands mixed up. She would have been in such horrible trouble if she had actually rung the bell.

The little old nuns and everyone else would have gotten up, dressed quickly, walked to the chapel and probably have prayed for a while before anyone realized it had been a terrible mistake. Juliette would have been thrown out that very morning. We would've never seen her again. When you got kicked out, nobody had a chance to say goodbye.

We would come to the study hall after Mass and breakfast for our daily instructions and there would be an empty desk, devoid of a name tag, notebooks and books. Sometimes it was announced. Often nothing was said. But we never knew why a fellow classmate had left. Did they leave on their own, or had they been kicked out? Most of the time we never knew. And a few days later the desk would be gone, and it would be like the person never even existed.

Juliette was sweating from more than the humidity. She put the bell down slowly on the gray linoleum floor, tiptoed back down the long dark corridor, hoping that she wouldn't run into S. Regina, who always seemed to be everywhere, even at night. Slipping into the dorm, she took her clothes off, put her nightgown on and went back to bed. She lay there sleepless for the rest of the night, listening to the wind and the rain, realizing how close she had been to getting thrown out.

Chapter 28
The Eye of the Beholder

It didn't take long for me to realize that S. Regina's thought processes were not the same as mine.

One morning in October a small group of us walked outside after breakfast, taking the usual path around the building--the only path around the building. I was suddenly aware of the beauty of the day. The air was cool and crisp. It had rained the night before and many beautiful gold, red and orange leaves had fallen. The sun was white and reflected silver on the river and big white cumulus clouds raced across the blue sky.

When we got to Bakery Square the concrete was covered with crimson and orange leaves. As we walked through them, a few of us picked up the leaves, each one prettier than the last. They reminded me of a Monet painting, with all the colors jumbled together. Every so often there was a splash of red or greenish orange, in contrast with the gray concrete underneath. I was the last one to come in the building. I took my black sweater off and carried it upstairs to the study hall, still thinking of the beauty of the autumn leaves.

S. Regina began talking about being mature enough to take responsibility for our actions and how far away we were from achieving that. Suddenly she stopped and got a half smile on her lips.

"Novices," she asked in what seemed to be a sudden change of heart, "who noticed the leaves on Bakery Square this morning as you came in from your walk?"

I couldn't believe she had noticed them. Maybe I was wrong about her. I thought she was so practical. I smiled as I realized that there is beauty and poetry hidden in all of us.

I raised my hand high, practically waving it in the air.

"Sister Susan, you noticed the leaves this morning?" S. Regina asked sweetly. I stood up.

"Yes, sister, I did." I was anxious to go on describing how beautiful they were but stopped as S. Regina's smile disappeared into the folds of her cheeks.

"And did you think about sweeping them up?" she

111

demanded.

I was standing very still. I heard myself saying, "No, sister," very softly.

"What did you say, sister?" she asked again.

I said, "No, sister," in a louder voice.

"You may sit down. This, novices, is exactly what I've been talking about." She looked over the whole group and kept talking.

"Sister Susan noticed the leaves this morning. She walked through the leaves this morning. But did she, did any of you, think about sweeping then up and disposing of them in the large trash can? No, of course not. Do you ever think of doing things on your own, sisters? Doing some chores that might relieve an older sister? No. This is what responsibility is, novices, and the day is coming when you won't have me around to remind you of your responsibilities."

"Sister Susan?" she addressed me again in her disappointed-beyond-all-belief voice.

"Yes," I said softly.

"You may sweep up bakery square after our instructions this morning. You may ask someone to help you, since all of you walked right through the leaves."

I sat at my desk through the rest of instructions, wondering how two people could inhabit the same world, see the same things, and interpret them in such a completely different way.

Instructions were over soon. I asked Clare, who was sitting right next to me, to help. We went down to the basement and asked Sister Godwin for two brooms. Then we proceeded to sweep up all the leaves.

When we finished, I leaned on the push broom and looked at the square. It was clean. The gray concrete looked darker in the damp morning, and a few ugly weeds poked up through the cracks. The leaves were squashed and buried in two big trash cans. Gone were the delicate reds and oranges, tinged with green, each leaf an object of art.

I knew S. Regina was right. The leaves needed to be swept up and I suppose we, the youngest ones, should do the job. But I was right too, and I knew that I didn't want my life to become gray and cold and without color like that ugly concrete square.

112

Chapter 29
Rules, Rules and More Rules

All I wanted was to be a good Christian. Most of the rules didn't have anything to do with Christianity. They were meaningless and reinforced the long-held patriarchal attitude of the church that we as sisters knew nothing.

For instance, the rule saying" Praise be to you, Lord Jesus Christ" seemed simple, but it put a formality into every greeting that didn't need to be there and set us all up for failure when we forgot to say it. We were then reminded by an older nun--any one of hundreds--that we had forgotten. It put us in a perpetual teacher-student relationship with everyone we met.

The rule about not talking to anyone outside of our small class was more insidious. I'm sure that it was made for a good reason a few centuries ago. The goal was to make our small group a real community of people who cared for each other, but making rules to achieve caring and concern in a small group just doesn't work. Force never teaches anyone anything.

I lived my life under a microscope, watched by someone all the time. Whenever I walked down the hall, laughing or even talking to someone, there was a fear of getting reported for being too loud or too immature. We had the unique privilege of being judged by everyone older and supposedly wiser than us.

Those were the simple rules--ones I learned to ignore as much as possible. It's not that I wanted to be a bad person, I just didn't ever see the relationship between most of the rules and Christianity. Being a Christian to me meant talking to people, caring for them, and helping them, and not this stiff cardboard formality that we tried so hard to achieve.

Some of the rules were completely insane. There was a rule that no sister could go in a boat. I pictured some saintly stout nun dressed in her heavy black shoes and serge dress, standing in a rowboat as the lake water lapped around her shoes. She wouldn't even try to swim--what good would that have done, weighed down by centuries of clothing.

I could see her hands clasped in prayer, sinking slowly till only bubbles remained. Sometimes I had too much meditation time

114

on my hands.

Then there was the rule about zithers. Our rule book said that we could not play zithers. I had to look up in my music book to find out what they were. It's a lute-like instrument. Perhaps it had heathenish sounds, or maybe some nun just played it badly, but there it was, prohibited in the rule book.

Then there were the rules that were truly heartbreaking and caused undue suffering and pain. There was a rule, recently changed when I entered, that stated a nun could only have two home visits in her lifetime. I knew many older nuns who would tell stories with tears in their eyes of how they could not go home to care for aged or dying parents because they wanted to save their visit for their parents' funerals.

This was all done in the name of Christianity. And I suppose the worst part of that rule changing in the early sixties was that the older nuns had to look on the new generation who could visit home many times and wonder what had been the purpose of all those rules? The sixties were a difficult time to be in religious life. The twenty-eight of us (we had already lost a few) knew the world we had left behind.

At least we knew it at the time we joined. We tried to keep up with the world, although it was difficult. The cut-up newspapers, the obsession with our own order and fake rules had very little to do with reality. Even though we had left that world behind, parts of it still seeped into our thinking and attitudes towards life.

We were not from a generation that accepted authority as being more knowledgeable. We were not a generation that liked to be told, "You'll understand when you're older."

And yet that's what we were told every day. I wanted to rebel--and I did. But not like Pam rebelled. Mine was quiet and sneaky, and very few people realized what I was doing. To outwardly rebel was to risk getting kicked out, and I wasn't ready to give up. In spite of everything being done to us, I was happy. Getting a good education, making friends, searching for God in my own way.

I didn't want to go to San Francisco and become a hippie who believed in free love and wore flowers in her hair.

Being friends with Maribeth and Joan was the sneakiest thing I had done--so far. That, and going up to the bell tower, but that was just a one-time event. When other nuns were around, I tried to be quiet and demure, never saying what I really thought.

I waded through the sludge and mud of the rules, following the ones I thought were important in terms of Christianity and morality. The rest I ignored as best I could, hoping there would come a time in the future when I could help change all of them for the better.

Chapter 30
The Not-So Divine Office

The fun and the pranks of the previous year were over. Study, instructions, and prayer occupied all our time. And our chores were no longer confined to the postulant's wing. They consisted of the jobs that nobody else wanted--we slaved in the heat of the laundry every week, cleaned the lavatories and chanted the divine office in front of the entire community in the big chapel. Luckily we took turns with that duty. One of us would stand in front of the entire congregation, leading the chanting for a whole week.

I had hoped at the beginning of the year that I might be overlooked or chosen for a permanent job like ringing the Angelus bell, but by January my time had come to do the one thing I feared most.

"Sister Dorothy, you will help the sisters in the kitchen. Sister Susan, you will chant the divine office next week in the big chapel."

I didn't hear any of the other assignments. My mind could only hear that one frightening sentence. Singing was one area where I didn't need humility. I was humble enough about it.

I could read music and I could stay on pitch. My voice was soft. In fact, it was so soft that when I opened my mouth I wasn't sure if anything would come out. I had never learned to sing because I played the piano. I was in every choir in grade school and high school, but as soon as the teachers found out I could play, I was literally on the bench for the entire year. And that was fine with me.

The thought of standing up in front of the congregation and singing terrified me. People assume if you're a musician, you can do anything musical. But it's like asking a violinist to play the clarinet in the orchestra on a moment's notice.

I practiced out in the fields behind the motherhouse, in the shower, softly in my bed at night. Monday morning dawned. I got up early and rushed to the refectory to down three hot cups of coffee. I fell in line with the novices as they sleepily walked to the chapel. I sat nervously at the end of the pew until S. Regina gave me "the look."

I stood shaking and walked to the front of the church and up to the microphone. I opened my mouth, "Praise the Lord..." but stopped. Nothing had come out. Maybe a little higher. "Praise the Lord." Still nothing. My last chance. Maybe a little lower. "Praise the Lord, O my soul." It was out. A half an octave lower than I had hoped, but it was out. I was so nervous I almost forgot the next line. The congregation answered properly. My mind fast-forwarded to the rest of the week. I could do it.

I jerked back to attention. There was silence in the chapel. I had lost my place. "The Lord is my shepherd." No response. I had chanted the wrong line. "Sing to the Lord a new song." No response.

S. Regina was getting up. She was walking to the front. She was next to me. I saw her finger over the words, I croaked, "Sing joyfully to the Lord all you on earth." The finger disappeared and the congregation finally answered. My heart started beating again. I kept my eyes down for the rest of the service. I kept them down at Mass, at breakfast, anytime I saw S. Regina that long day, waiting for the inevitable, "Sister Susan, would you come into my office?"

But it never came. I don't know why, and I never lost my place again that whole week. But I would have given anything to clean toilets instead for the rest of the year.

Chapter 31
The Artists

When we moved on to the novitiate, a new group of postulants entered and took over our old section of the building.

One of the postulants was a musician, and I heard from my piano teacher that she played the violin beautifully. She had played with the Seattle Symphony when she was twelve years old, so she had to be quite accomplished.

I knew there had to be a way for us to play together. I just didn't know how. The novitiate rules were so strict. Once a month we had an hour-long recreation with the postulants. Other than that, we could never speak to them at all. I introduced myself to her at the next month's recreation, and Louise and I decided to try and get together to play. Our music teacher thought it was a great idea, but we had to get it past S. Beatrice and S. Regina, two people not known for their creative and innovative spirits.

I knocked on S. Regina's door one morning, summoning up what little courage I had. Even though I thought I was smart and had some pretty good ideas, S. Regina could siphon out any courage, hope, and creativity just with one withering look.

"Yes?" she answered, looking up. When she saw me, her smile disappeared into the maze of wrinkles and folds of her face.

I stood in front of her desk, trying to phrase my outlandish request in the most humble, penitential manner, like I was asking God for a big favor.

"Uh, S. Regina, Sister Verene told me about a new postulant who plays the violin, and I was wondering if we could get permission to practice together and give a concert. S. Verene hoped we could." There! I spit it out. I knew it was hopeless, but at least I had tried.

S. Regina looked at me like I had just asked the pope to become an atheist and said, "Why would you want to do that?"

I grabbed onto my chance like a lifeboat.

"Well, sister, I think it would be good to share what we're learning in the music department with both our communities."

Wow! I managed to get community, sharing and education all in one sentence. I was pleased with myself.

"I'm not saying no--yet--but don't plan on it." She waved me away and picked up some papers.

A few weeks later, S. Regina called me during our study hall. "Sister Susan, come in here!"

I couldn't imagine what I had done wrong this time. There was so much to choose from. Actually, there used to be so much to choose from. Not anymore. My rule-breaking had been dealt some serious blows in the novitiate. I had no opportunity and no time to do anything wrong, although the desire was as strong as ever.

"Sister Beatrice and I have decided that you and that postulant can practice together--only for this one concert. After that, no more. You may practice two times a week. S. Verene will help coordinate your schedules. And see that you practice, not talk!"

"Yes, sister," I replied, and scooted out of the office before she could take it all back.

Louise and I had great fun together. It's always a joy to work with an excellent musician. We could both sight-read almost all the music, and we decided on a mix of contemporary and classical music that we hoped would entertain everyone. We did talk a little, but most of the time we spent doing what we loved-- making music.

The evening of the recital came. Both our classes made up the audience. We played and we played well. As I sat there at the piano, I tried to concentrate on the music, but part of me realized that this was what music was all about. Giving enjoyment to others and sharing it with them.

The auditorium with its beautiful grand piano was almost full. Our music teacher sat in the front row. Louise and I played a Bach piece, then a part of a Mozart Sonata for violin and piano, then Bruch, and ended with Copland.

I loved performing. I was aware of the lights on the stage and how the sound felt strong even with so many in the room. I glanced out the window at the bare trees as the sound of the violin and piano blended together seamlessly.

Then it was over. I smiled as I heard the clapping of the group and hoped we could do this again. Our recital was during one of our recreation periods, and I know a lot of the novices were

120

glad to get out of folk dancing or basketball, which we did almost every evening.

S. Verene was in the front row, clapping loudly after each piece. She was usually quite careful and reserved in her praise, but tonight she looked so proud of us--her students!

We were asked to perform one more piece, so we chose "Meditation" by Massenet, a very popular piece--in classical music circles.

After the concert, Louise and I talked for a few minutes as we put away our music out in the hall.

"That was great!" I told her, smiling from ear to ear.

"Yeah, I think everybody enjoyed it. I hope we can do it again soon. Let's think about new pieces!" We had become good friends in the time we had practiced together. We had talked, but mostly just enjoyed the thrill of playing together.

I hugged her quickly and we both headed down the long corridor to our respective sections of the building. S. Verene came up from behind us. "Hold on! I just wanted to tell you both that you did an amazing job. Just beautiful. I'm so proud of you both."

I said, "Thank you, sister," and so did Louise. For the first time in months, I felt the satisfaction of doing a good job--and especially for and in front of my classmates. We had very little opportunity for concerts or any cultural events and I hoped Louise and I could fill in that gap just a little.

I got back to the novitiate. Everyone was already studying. I sat down at my desk. Juliette walked by and whispered, "Wow, that was really great!" Ruth smiled and gave me a thumbs up. Pam waved from the back of the room. Even Kathy smiled at me.

S. Regina appeared at the door of her office. "Sister Susan, come here."

I jumped up happily, still in the glow of the concert.

"In here," she motioned to her office.

I stood in front of her desk as she walked behind it and sat down. The door to the office was wide open.

I smiled. I knew I had done a good job and knew that Regina would be pleased. I didn't think she would appreciate the music that much, but she could give credit to hard work and achievement.

She looked straight at me and said, "You and that postulant think you're special, don't you?"

I wasn't quite sure what she meant, but her face was red and ugly looking.

"No sister, we're not special," I replied, confused. I didn't quite understand what she was saying. Had we done something wrong that I hadn't even noticed? She had given us permission to play. She knew what we were doing.

"You think you're better than everyone else here because you play music, don't you?"

"No, I don't…" I started to answer but she cut me off.

"I was ashamed of you tonight, getting up there and showing off, showing how much better you are than anyone else here, how you're so special," she said with great bitterness.

"What? I don't understand, sister." Tears were welling up in my eyes. I didn't want to cry but I couldn't help it. I truly couldn't understand what she was talking about.

"No, I think you understand very well. Asking for special privileges to practice and give this concert. No one else could do that and get away with it. If you want to be a member of this order you had better get rid of the idea that you're better than everyone else!"

I stood quietly, not saying a word, but inside I was getting angrier every second. How dare she take something that was beautiful, a gift that God had given to me, and ruin it like this--not only for me--but for everyone in my class. I kept praying to God that she would stop, but God was nowhere to be found.

I looked at her hands, wrinkled and red, flat on the desktop. I hated them. I hated her.

"You have no idea of the meaning of humility, standing up there and performing while people clapped and clapped. You thought you were better than anyone else, didn't you?"

She kept repeating herself.

I kept saying, "No, sister." I looked at the dark window behind her. I could only see my reflection, standing there, pale and blurred.

She had to stop soon. What else could she possibly say? I felt like I was in a dream. She was yelling now, repeating the same

122

things over and over. How I had no humility, that getting up and performing in front of people was disgusting and full of pride. How I better learn to be humble, or I would be thrown out of the order quickly. How pride was a sin in the eyes of God. I thought of my classmates, listening intently from the other room.

"You are so close to getting thrown out of this congregation." I was shocked when she said that. I had no idea I was "close" to getting thrown out. I thought I was doing a pretty good job trying to be a nun. It wasn't easy, especially with all the stupid rules that got in the way.

"I'm warning you that people like you, who think they're better than everyone else, will not make it in this order. You had better think long and hard about yourself and if you think you are really suited for this kind of life. I was never more embarrassed than to see both of you parading in front of everyone."

And then she sputtered to a stop, like a car running out of gas, and she yelled, "Get out. Just get out!"

I remember walking back to my desk, putting my books away and just standing there, not knowing what to do next. A few people were staring at me--most were looking down at their desks, trying not to make eye contact. I left the room and walked up the stairs, tears blurring everything. I could barely make it up the four flights. I had to stop and catch my breath. I couldn't let anyone see me crying, but luckily there was no one around. I heard the grandfather clock dimly chime down below in the corridor.

I got to the dormitory, pulled the tan curtains closed, shutting myself off from the rest of the dorm, and sat on my bed for a while. I took off my ugly shoes and put them to the side.

Louise and I had done a wonderful job. To be yelled at like that was beyond my comprehension.

I hated her so much. I hated this place. I hated that she had the power to do that to me.

I would call my parents in the morning and leave. I couldn't take this anymore. I took off my clothes, one by one, put on my nightgown and remembered to go quickly to the bathroom before anyone else came upstairs. I didn't want to talk to anyone-- or even see anyone. I came back and sat on my bed staring at the ugly curtains for a long time.

There was something inside me that broke that night, but there was also something else that started growing in me. Something solid and hard that couldn't be touched or broken anymore. I was right and I knew it. She could say whatever she wanted but I knew she was wrong.

I didn't sleep at all that night. Thoughts kept spinning through my head. How much I hated her--and I still had most of the year with her--whether this was all worth it--to be humiliated like that and still go on. How could I?

I thought about what she had said--that I thought I was so special. Yes, I did think I was special because God gave me a talent that I had worked hard to perfect. Every musician has to want to perform in front of people--to "show off" in her ugly words. That's what music was about. It was about sharing with other people. That's what gave life and meaning to musicians--to be able to share that gift with others.

That hard spot kept growing all that night amid the tears. I knew I was right, that I was ok, that I was talented, that I wanted to do the right thing, and she wasn't going to take that away from me. I would not let her take that away from me!

I had my studies, my friends that I had made, my hope for the future. She tried hard to break me, but she couldn't take that away.

I didn't leave the next day. I'm not sure why. Maybe it was because I was a coward, but I still had this unwavering belief that things would get better--the eternal optimist in me. It was hard seeing her the next morning and all the mornings after that. I hated what she had done to me and to Louise. I felt I was ruined in my classmate's estimation. There were a lot of them who took her opinions very seriously.

Her words stayed with me for a long time. I never talked about that night to any of my classmates, except a few words with Pam and Juliette, who tried to understand but had their own problems to deal with.

The next day I saw S. Verene. She said, "I was so proud of you and Louise last night. You did a wonderful job. I hope you can do it again. Pick out some more pieces and maybe you both can give a concert next semester, or even sooner, if you have the time."

I tried to smile. "Thanks, I'll start looking for some new pieces."

"I will too," S.Verene said brightly. "I'll put them with your music."

I couldn't ever bring myself to tell her what had happened. She would have been furious, but I was a coward. I didn't want her to confront Regina because of the repercussions I might receive.

I never talked to Louise about it either. I didn't want her to know how horrible S. Regina might treat her the next year. I kept it all inside, but what had been such joy and freedom in my life became filled with tension, worry, and an ever-present guilt about what had once been my greatest accomplishment.

Chapter 32
The Tree of Life

I stumbled through the next few weeks, trying to reconcile my bitterness toward S. Regina with my future as a nun. What made everything worse was the seeming lack of sympathy from my classmates. They had all heard what S. Regina had said, but no one said anything to me. I received a few worried and concerned looks, but everyone had their own novitiate-related problems to deal with. And there wasn't any chance to talk freely--or to talk at all. I felt like I was in solitary confinement.

One morning after instructions I got up and walked outside the study hall past S. Regina's office. There was a large potted plant in front of her door and Juliette stood next to it, practically hiding behind it.

"What are you doing?" I whispered. "What is it?"

"My mom and dad sent it to me. It's a rubber tree--plant--I don't know. It has my name on it. Regina's going to kill me. What am I going to do with it?"

S. Regina must have heard us talking and walked angrily out the door. Most of the novices walking in the hall scattered like cockroaches, leaving Juliette and me standing guiltily by her tree.

"Sister, what is this thing?" S. Regina sounded confused. She didn't seem to know if Juliette had done something bad, so it wasn't her usual scathing tone.

"Sister, my parents sent it to me. It's a rubber tree."

"And just what are you going to do with it?" S. Regina was warming up to her usual nasty tone of voice.

Juliette stood meekly looking at the floor. I knew she was trying to find the correct answer but didn't realize yet that there wasn't a correct answer.

"Uh," she started badly. Then she looked up at S. Regina.

"Sister, we could put it in the refectory?" She looked back down at her shoes.

S. Regina rose quickly to her five feet, seven inches of authority.

"YOU may put it in the refectory, Sister Juliette. And it is your responsibility to take care of it."

126

"Don't let it die," she added loudly as she walked back to her office. I offered to help Juliette carry the tree downstairs to our novitiate dining room.

We lugged the tree downstairs and into the room.

She stood looking at the tree.

"I don't know where to put it," she said dejectedly, wiping her forehead. That tree was heavy.

"Well, just put it in the corner over there," I said, anxious to get back upstairs to do my cleaning. And I didn't really want to have anything to do with the rubber tree. I had enough problems of my own.

"I don't know."

"It's just a plant--or tree. It doesn't matter, "I said quickly to hurry her along.

"Ok, ok, the corner is good." We moved it and turned its best side toward the room.

"I just hope it doesn't die," Juliette sighed as we walked back upstairs.

"Don't worry about it," I told her. She had enough responsibilities already. She was having a hard time keeping herself neat, getting her work done, trying not to talk, and she still managed to attract trouble like a magnet. She didn't need to take on something new.

We ate in the refectory three times a day. It was on the ground floor of the building but most of it was below the ground. It had high windows, so there was some small light that filtered in. There was nothing except white-washed bare walls and S. Regina's droning voice to concentrate on. Every day she read about a saint from a big volume, "The Lives of the Saints." None of the saints had anything in common with us, and her words were just like a mosquito in my ear. I was glad when the humming of her voice stopped. We were never tested on the readings. They were just there as a background to the clinking of forks and glasses around the room.

The food was excellent. House sisters worked in the Big Kitchen all day, preparing the meals for the huge motherhouse. Cooking for three to four hundred people was unimaginable to me. Some weeks I had kitchen duty and two of us would take the carts of empty pots and pans back after we ate, rolling them down the long corridor to the kitchen. There we spent the next hour with the students from the other classes washing all the cookware in huge industrial steel sinks. We couldn't speak to them, and when we had kitchen duty we missed our evening recreation, but we could talk to the novice working alongside us, so it wasn't that bad. Usually it would be dark when we finished cleaning, leaving the big kitchen sparkling, ready for the next mornings cooking.

One day at lunch I noticed that a few big leaves had fallen off the rubber plant. It still had plenty, though, and it didn't look sick.

I was right next to Juliette on the morning walk. "Is that rubber plant supposed to lose its leaves?" I asked innocently.

Juliette looked at me in despair. "I don't know. I'm watering it and I think it's okay. Maybe it's not getting enough light. Oh gosh, I can't let it die. S. Regina will kill me!" Joanne and Ellen joined us so we didn't talk anymore about the plant.

I'm sure the plant would have thrived better in the jungles of the Philippines. It needed a tropical climate and probably wasn't getting enough sunlight, warmth, or water to do very well.

At least once a day I'd notice the rubber plant. It was the only living thing in the room besides us and was about as lively.

We sat like the statues in the halls. I found myself glancing at the rubber tree more often. There was no mistaking it now. It was beginning to look bad. I wondered if that tree somehow represented my life. Starting off religious life fresh and green, and then from lack of water and sunlight, gradually starting to die.

The morning came when the rubber tree had only one leaf. I was still hoping for the best. It would have to be an actual miracle at this point. I glanced at Juliette sitting across from me, but she was staring despondently at her grapefruit.

With one leaf it could recover and flourish, possibly even stage a resurrection scenario which we were all familiar with--at least in theory. Was my religious life down to one leaf? I found myself praying for the one leaf. Juliette was probably so sick of the rubber tree that she prayed for its quick demise.

S. Regina's droning voice went on about where the saint had been born, why she had become so holy at such an early age,

128

how good it was to be both a virgin and a martyr, like that was something we were all looking forward to.

The meal was finally over. We stood up, cleared away the grapefruit rinds and the empty oatmeal bowls, washed and dried the dishes, but S. Regina kept reading. We all sat down again. I looked at the rubber tree framed against the white wall. It was only a stick now, with its one leaf holding on tenaciously.

We waited for S. Regina to realize that we had all finished breakfast. No one would dare say anything to her. We had to get together in this very room once a month to discuss our faults in front of everyone, and no one wanted to confess how they had interrupted the novice mistress, so we all sat and waited.

Finally, S. Regina stopped reading, lifted up her eyes, and took a breath. And then it happened. With an audible plop, the last leaf on the rubber tree fell to the floor.

A novice at the end of the room chuckled, and then another. Rachel put her hand to her mouth. I had to hold my lips tightly together or I'd start giggling. Up and down the table a flood of laughter welled up in us. The laughing got louder.

Suddenly S. Regina stood up and glared at us.

"Novices!" she said sternly. Whatever had seemed so funny a second ago didn't seem funny anymore.

"Sister Juliette?" S. Regina called out loudly. Juliette stood up, heavy on her tiny feet.

"You had the responsibility for this plant?"

"Yes, sister," Juliette whispered meekly.

"You have obviously not taken care of it properly."

"Yes, sister," Juliette whispered more softly.

"If you can't take care of a simple plant, Sister Juliette, how do you ever expect to take care of those children and adults who will be entrusted to your care?" Her eyes held their unflinching stare at poor Juliette.

"I don't know, sister," Juliette could barely speak. Tears came to her eyes.

"You may remove the dead plant today, Sister." And S. Regina stood up and strode to the door, her book in her hand.

I looked at Juliette who was still standing, looking at the lifeless plant.

"Do you need some help?" I asked as I walked over to her.

"No, that's ok," she answered sadly. "I can do it myself."

I walked outside alone that morning, still thinking about the rubber tree. I had hope for my life after the motherhouse. But another three years might be too long to survive this endless winter, where no warmth or sunlight seemed to penetrate.

Chapter 33
Conversation 101

Pam drew the short straw when we changed our cleaning duties and had to clean the novice's study hall, including S. Regina's office.

"Why couldn't I clean the toilets, like Marjorie? Why did I have to get HER office?" Pam moaned on the way to class.

"I don't know," I sympathized.

My chore was to clean the main staircase in the center of the building, all four stories of it. Hundreds of steps, but the worst parts were the ornately carved balusters that lined the staircase. There were hundreds of them, each curve designed to hold the maximum amount of dust.

I was lucky though to be alone on the staircase. Pam would have rather done anything than be in such close proximity to S.Regina in her office.

"I'll have to be in her office every day now," she sighed. "I'm in there often enough I might as well clean it, I guess."

On our evening walk a few weeks later, Pam came up behind me quickly. "I have to tell you what happened today."

"Are you okay?"

There was always the fear the Pam would get kicked out and I'd never see her again.

"Yeah, I'm okay. I was in Regina's office this afternoon dusting. She walked in and gave me this sour look. You know how good she is at that."

I nodded.

"She couldn't say anything, though, because I'm supposed to be there! And I'm doing a good job. So I'm down on the floor, dusting the baseboards, and Regina says to me, 'I've been thinking about that request of yours, sister.' "

"I said, 'Which request, sister?'

She said 'Yes, I think it would be a good idea.'

Boy, was I confused. I just kept staring at the baseboards, trying to think of what request I had made, but I couldn't think of any.

So I just said, 'Ok, sister, thanks. I'll be glad to do it.' I mean, if I had requested something, it must have been something I wanted to do, so that was great. That's never happened before. I couldn't believe it. And I said thank you again.'

'Next Tuesday would be the best time,' Regina said. And she said it so sweetly.

'So I said, 'Ok, that'll work for me.' She'd never talked to me this much--ever. And she was real nice about it, not like she usually is.

Then she said, 'I'll be looking forward to it.'

And she was so kind sounding, not her usual bitter, nasty self.

I really tried to remember what she was talking about, but I just couldn't figure it out. I was almost done with the baseboards and ready to get up. Then I heard a loud click and she says,

'Sister Pamela, get up and look at me.' She sounded completely different, angry and upset, you know, her usual self.

I jumped up with that dust rag in my hand.

Then she starts yelling at me, 'Sister Pamela, I was ON THE TELEPHONE--talking to S. Alphonse, the head of this entire order. I was not speaking to YOU--the conversation had nothing to do with you. Are you that unaware of what is going on around you?'

I said, 'No sister, I mean, yes, sister, I guess so sister.' I didn't know what to say by that time."

She kept going. 'You had no business listening in on a private conversation of mine, much less being so oblivious that you didn't even know it was not directed to you. Come over here. Right now.'

So I had to walk over to her desk, wondering how long it was going to take. She had me in there for at least a half hour. But hey, I'm still here."

"Oh Pam, you should've known. First of all, she was nice."

"Yeah…I guess."

"Secondly, she wanted to do something that you had asked for…"

"Yeah…well, that's true. Like that was ever going to happen…"

We reached the door to go inside. I put my hand on her

132

shoulder. "And third, I'm sure glad you're still here."

"Yeah...I guess I'm lucky. That makes maybe the hundredth time." She smiled as we walked inside.

"At least the hundredth," I whispered mostly to myself.

Chapter 34
Laundry Day

The Catholic Church taught that there were seven virtues and practicing them was a good way to avoid the seven deadly sins. Humility was the virtue that combatted pride, and we had many instruction periods devoted to humility. We had taken vows of Poverty, chastity and obedience, but those weren't quite enough. We had to add all those other virtues to be considered holy enough to be sisters.

We had to confess our faults in front of the whole group. That didn't happen too often--I think it was one of those outdated rules that was on its way out. But I do remember being humiliated a few times. S. Regina was a master at humiliation, even more so than S. Beatrice.

Many of our lessons had to do with our attitudes toward other people. We were the college students getting our fancy degrees. But we were taught that anything we did, if we did it for God, was worthwhile. That included all the house sisters; the cooks, the seamstresses, the sisters who worked in the laundry, and the hundreds of "house" sisters out on mission who took care of the convents.

I remember S. Godwin clearly. She was a tall thin nun in her sixties at least, and she was the baker for the entire motherhouse. She had to get up at an even more ungodly hour than the rest of us and start baking bread. I respected her a lot and appreciated all she did for us. I know I had a lot of pride in me, but I have always admired people like her who work hard in menial jobs.

I knew we would be praying a lot more as novices, but I wasn't prepared for doing the laundry for the entire motherhouse. We'd go downstairs every Thursday to a huge boiler room with whitewashed walls. Industrial machines filled the room and the steam from the long rollers on the machines in the center rose up and covered everything in a hot fog.

Janice and I usually worked on the sheets. Two other novices would feed wet sheets into the hungry steaming machine, and after a few contortions they would come out hot, white and dry

134

from the other side into our four waiting hands. Then fold, grab, walk toward each other, grab one end, walk back, fold and fold again and lay them carefully in the neatly stacked pile. By then the next sheet was relentlessly rolling its way out. We'd usually work for four hours at a time. No visits to the bathroom, no friendly chatting over the roar of the machines, not even time to blow my nose. The only times that were bearable were chilly winter days when the heat felt almost welcoming. In the summer, however, we would trudge over to the laundry room in our long serge habits. The temperature might be approaching a hundred degrees outside. Nobody wanted to guess what the temperature was inside as we dripped our way through the afternoon.

In our instruction periods upstairs we learned that we weren't special. I had my own personal lesson from S. Regina when I gave my music concert. We never had any lectures on building self-esteem. But we did have a lot of hours devoted to overcoming pride and selfishness. I don't remember much from my lessons in instructions, but I learned a lot more in the laundry room. I learned humility, perseverance, and an appreciation for those sisters who did the hard work while we sat back and learned from our books. It was a lesson in humility--and humidity--that I never forgot.

Chapter 35
The Webers

One morning I picked up what was left of the paper. We were still reading an abridged version of the St. Louis Post-Dispatch, probably minus sex, provocative ads and stories. I'll never really know what we missed. And we had even less access to the television. Once a week or so we were permitted to watch the news, but only if there was something of great importance.

That morning I looked at page four of the local headlines and couldn't believe what I saw.

"Mafia blamed for St. Louis lawyer's death."

A close friend of our family, John Weber, had been shot 47 times and his body dumped in the ocean off the coast of Florida.

I just stared at the article. My sister Carol had been life-long friends with Julia, his daughter. They met in grade school and continued to be close friends in high school. Carol had even worked for John as his secretary for years. He had so much money that he even gave her a used car so she could get to and from work easily.

We always assumed he was a good honest person, but apparently there was another side to him that none of us knew about. I didn't know much about the Mafia, but I knew it existed in St. Louis and controlled a lot of the city. Getting shot forty-seven times and being dumped in the ocean sounded like something I had seen in crime dramas--before I entered the convent. Maybe that's how John had made a lot of his money, although I can't imagine that my sister didn't know about his dealings with the Mafia. She worked for him but she wouldn't have been involved in anything like that. It was very confusing.

I thought back to the first time I had ever met him. We had all been invited to his house for a barbeque. I couldn't have been more than seven years old.

My parents, with Carol and I in the back seat, pulled off the highway onto a two-lane paved road through a forested area outside of St. Louis. Through the grey ghostlike trees I could see the Missouri River. Then we came to a gate. Carol jumped out of the car and opened the gate with a numbered code and we continued on past the pastures where beautiful horses grazed. We came to a huge home.

"Wow," I said, never having seen anything quite so beautiful, but Carol laughed and said, "Sue, those are just the stables!" I was embarrassed, but they were huge and expensive looking with a large courtyard in front. There were horses in the courtyard, and what looked like little homes above the stables with windows. It was elegant to me, with its red tiled roof.

We drove down past the tennis courts my dad had been talking about. He was dressed in his tennis shorts and shirt with his racket in the trunk, ready to play. John had always wanted to play tennis with my father, who had been Missouri State champion the year I was born.

John became very interested in the sport and told Carol that maybe if he had his own tennis courts, my dad would play with him. So that's what he did. He built two tennis courts. They looked very cool now--it was spring, but I imagined in the summer they would get very hot, out in the sun with no trees around them.

We reached the end of the circular drive and there was a stone house. It didn't look all that big, but as I got out of the car, I realized I was level with the top floor of the house, and there were more floors underneath, three I found out later, hidden and built into the huge stone bluffs.

It was a fairy tale house to me. We walked in and saw a hallway that had Oriental carpeting and plush furniture lining the walls. And we hadn't even gotten to a room yet! Each floor of the house was four times bigger than our house, and I wandered from room to room exploring in amazement--with Mom's permission, of course. The lower floor was all kitchen and eating areas. The second floor was living rooms and parlors and expensive red sofas made with velvet. I touched a red velvet sofa and then pulled my hand away afraid I would leave a mark on it. Antiques crowded the coffee tables and beautiful pictures in gold frames lined the walls. I was too afraid to sit down. I just peeked into most of the rooms from the doorways. On the third floor were closed doors, probably to bedrooms. I didn't dare open those doors. And out in front was a rock wall which bordered the forest and the river down below. Off the patio in the shade of hundreds of oak trees was the pool, green and still cold in the spring, filled with tiny green frogs. I loved watching them, doing their genuine frog kicks across the surface of the pool. Swimming with them was even more fun, coming up for air and seeing a frog in my face. I always opened my eyes and checked before I took a breath of air.

John and his family were the richest people I had ever known. I couldn't even imagine having that amount of money.

I can't remember how many times we drove out to the huge house, but I remember the first time I saw the stars. I was a city girl and had never been on a vacation. The only stars I had ever seen were from my backyard- the Big Dipper and Venus and Mars and a few others in the night sky. We were driving home late at night along the Missouri River from the Webers when I was still a little girl and I put my head back in the rear-view window and looked up into the sky. There were no lights at all except our car lights, and I saw a million stars in the clear sky. I had never seen them before. The whiteness of the Milky Way spilled across the sky, and I saw clusters of stars and constellations I had only seen in books, spread out over the night sky. It was the most beautiful thing I had ever seen. We turned onto a city road and the lights in the sky gradually faded away as the streetlights glared through the windows. It was years before I saw the night sky again.

One afternoon years later, I was in my teens by this time, my dad and John came back inside from playing tennis, and his daughter Julia walked in.

"Dad, the red car is missing and I need to use it."

John looked up at her. "Nobody has it, baby. Go out and look for it again."

Julia came back a few minutes later, her mouth in a pout, looking a little annoyed. "Dad, somebody forgot to put on the parking brake and it went off the cliff. I can see it down in the trees from the driveway."

She crossed her arms in frustration and stood looking at her dad expectantly.

John just looked back at her and shrugged his shoulders.

"Well, take Marge's car, then. That's still there, isn't it?"

I stood there in amazement that people could have so much money that they wouldn't even care if one of their cars had fallen

138

off a cliff. We had one car and would have been devastated if anything had ever happened to it. We would buy one every ten years or so, when my parents had saved up enough money.

John once said to my dad, "You're the only real friend I have." My dad told us that over dinner one evening, feeling really bad because he never considered John to be a close friend. But my father was the one person who didn't care how much money John had, and apparently was one of the few who had never asked him for money.

After John was killed, his widow and family had no money left. They sold the home and moved away. My sister Carol had been shocked to discover John's shady dealings with the Mafia because she knew nothing about it when she worked for him. Once, years later as adults, my sister Carol and I drove back to the old home when I was in St. Louis. I wanted to know if it was as I remembered it, or if it was just a child's fantasy.

We drove along the old river road and pulled up to the gate. We couldn't get through it any longer, since it was owned by someone else, but I could see the old stables. There were no horses in the field, and although I got out of the car and looked, I couldn't see that childhood memory any longer. It was hidden by the forest.

I thought of how lucky I was. I had my parents and sisters. They were good honest people who enjoyed life. I had my family. That was my wealth. I felt sorry for John, knowing that people cared for him only for his money.

Years later, Carol called me one day when I was living in California.

"Hey Sue, remember John Weber?"

"Sure."

"Well, you'll be interested in this."

"What?"

"There was an article in the St. Louis Post-Dispatch this morning about him. Apparently, he wasn't as bad as we all thought. The reason he was murdered was because he was going to testify AGAINST the Mafia."

"No kidding!"

"I mean, I know that he worked with them, but in the end, he was at least trying to do the right thing, and that must have been why he got killed."

Carol and I talked a little longer about him and what had become of his family, but after we hung up, I realized that I had thought badly about him all those years, and that he had died trying to at least do some good.

What a sad way to live, though. Wondering if people were your friends, or if they just cared about your money.

Chapter 36
Reality Class

The first week of January, S. Regina passed out our class schedule for the spring semester. I quickly looked over the list. There wasn't much besides instructions and prayers, but we were all required to take a class called "Reality."

Pam walked out in the hall with me. "What's this "reality" class?"

"I don't know. It must have something to do with theology, or we wouldn't be taking it."

When we went to the first class, we discovered it was a philosophy class, dealing with some of the great philosophers in history. It had a definite Catholic slant, with St. Thomas Aquinas and St. Augustine prominent in our readings.

I was interested in Teilhard de Chardin, the popular and liberal Catholic philosopher who was still alive and writing. but we didn't get that far. We got stuck in the 13th century. We definitely didn't read Camus or Neitzsche or Schopenhauer, those philosophers who didn't think much of God. Atheists were not part of the agenda.

All of us novices took the class, taught by S. Winifred, who was about eighty or so, give or take a few centuries.

We were only two weeks into the spring semester and Pam and I were walking around the building on our evening recreation. Everybody else had gone in because of the cold, but we had about fifteen minutes left, and we decided to go around one more time, even though the cold February wind was blowing hard.

"What do you think about our "reality" class?" Pam asked with a smile.

"Yeah, reality. I think it's kind of ridiculous to talk about "reality" in here."

Pam laughed. "Look at me." She spun around, her long habit twirling around her skinny legs, her frizzy hair sticking out of the veil, as usual.

"This is definitely NOT reality," she laughed.

I started laughing too. "And the fact that there are no men except ancient priests…"

Pam interrupted me, "Don't forget the mysterious men in the basement!"

"Yeah, and a ridiculous rule of silence, and an old lady telling us what to do and think every day. And our clothes! This isn't reality! It's not even a very good fantasy!"

Pam jumped back in, "And laundry duty and prayers. Oh my God, all the prayers. I think I'm about all prayed out."

"And the newspaper cuttings and getting yelled at once or twice a day."

By this time we were both laughing so hard we were crying.

"What if I get an "A" in the class? Does that mean I've lost my sense of reality?" I could barely breathe, I was laughing so hard.

"Are you kidding?" Pam whispered, since we were getting close to the door. "It doesn't matter what grade we get. We've lost all sense of reality just by being here."

Pam and I tried to wipe the smiles off our faces as we walked in the door. Whatever smile remained disappeared when I saw S. Regina waiting at the end of the corridor for us, probably wondering what we were smiling about.

I got a "B" in my "reality" class. And I only got that because I cheated on the final exam. Yes, I was a nun, and I copied the answers to two questions from the sister next to me. She probably didn't know any more about "reality" than I did.

It was the only time I ever cheated on a test and my cheating didn't even help, because the B brought down my grade point average. I suppose I deserved it.

But I still laugh when I think about our class in "reality." I'm glad I didn't get an "A."

142

Chapter 37
Martin Luther King

April, 1968

One piece of news we did hear about quickly, even though we were in the novitiate, was the assassination of Reverend Martin Luther King. It didn't have much relevance to me inside the walls of the convent, but I knew it was terrible for the whole country, and possibly the whole future of civil rights, to lose a man of that greatness.

I could see the pain in Pam's eyes. She needed to be at home with her family, talking about it, being a part of her black community. Instead she was in a white world, an insulated old white German world that might know about civil rights but didn't much care.

I don't mean that the church didn't care about social justice. Many of the priests and bishops in South and Central America were leading the great social reforms. And the teachers in our own order cared about the poor and the neglected. That's why we were there. To help the people who needed help.

But the motherhouse was conservative and had one purpose--to train us as nuns and teachers. We didn't spend a lot of time on social justice. And since it was an old German order, nobody knew anything about black communities and their concerns.

Pam and I talked about Reverend King, but what could I say? I had no idea of what it was like to be black and to have a man of such importance killed. My only experience was with John Kennedy, but he didn't represent a struggling minority in our country. We talked, and I knew Pam was heartbroken and frustrated and struggling to stay.

I felt there was still hope, though, in Robert Kennedy, and I followed his campaign as much as I could. Kennedy managed to stay in our edited newspaper, since the campaign had nothing to do with sex. I was hoping against hope that he would be the next Democratic presidential candidate. I remember the day of the California primary, June 1968, sitting on the edge of my seat all day in class, wondering if he would win. And then the poll results started to come in. They let us have the television on in the study hall.

He won the primary. I was so excited. He could be the next president! There was still a chance to regain some hope for our beleaguered country.

And then just as quickly we heard the news. He was dead. It was all over. And I remember seeing that picture of him lying on the floor of the Ambassador Hotel, all our dreams dead with him. John Kennedy's death affected all of us in the country: I'll never forget those days of unbelievable sadness and anger, but Robert Kennedy's death affected me more. It was the death of hope. Even now, in 2021, I can't read a book about him, I can't see that picture of him on the tile floor of the hotel, I can't watch any old news clips or speeches of his without feeling that same inexpressible sadness of what almost was--what could have been.

Chapter 38
The Crown of Thorns

I remember that it was March--the front lawn turned from bare black sticks of trees to a beautiful wash of green all the way down to the railroad tracks and the Mississippi river beyond. Clover was everywhere and dandelions sprouted through the grass. We had just come inside from our morning walk, heading down the corridor, our loud voices fading into nothingness as we approached the study hall.

We found our seats as usual and waited for S. Regina and our morning instructions. As the clock chimed eight times, she walked in the room and up to the podium.

"Novices, I have something special to tell you today. As you know, you will be professing your vows this summer at the St. Louis Cathedral, and in preparation for that you will be making a crown of thorns to wear over your veils. This is a symbol of your religious life, of the suffering you may someday have to endure because of your belief in Christ, and a remembrance of Christ's suffering for our sins."

"You may enhance the crown tastefully, in your own creative ways, and you will all wear the crowns proudly as junior sisters on that special day. You will want to make them look beautiful, since you will be wearing them in front of everyone."

"You will also have a wooden crown box to keep the crown of thorns in forever as a reminder of your commitment to Christ."

My heart sank as I heard her talk. What a stupid and ridiculous idea. We had heard for two years about the suffering that we as Christians, and especially nuns, might have to endure when we went out in today's horrible, secular world. I wasn't very concerned that was going to happen.

Our lives were wonderful compared to most people. We got three meals a day, a place to live, good medical care, and a free education. We had to give up some things, and got yelled at a lot, but there were billions of people in the world who had a more difficult life than we did. There were people starving, who had no place to live, had to endure terrible diseases, and we were the ones who were going to wear a crown of thorns as a symbol of our difficult life? It seemed ludicrous and I hated it.

I never really found it inspiring to think about the suffering and death of Christ. I wanted to be a joyful Christian, a real messenger of the 'good news,' and making a crown of thorns didn't appeal to me in the slightest.

I wondered why I was so against the idea one morning during meditation. Most of the other novices seemed okay, or at least resigned to it. I watched the light filter in through the stained-glass windows around the altar, the rich blues and reds spreading wider across the marble floor. My eyes wandered to the statue of Mary in the corner and suddenly I remembered someone from elementary school.

She had a round face, brown hair, and her name was Marjorie Thompson. She had long eyelashes and was always scrubbed with rosy cheeks. Pretty ribbons wove through her hair, and she wore large bracelets made of colored glass. She was every teacher's pet from kindergarten to eighth grade.

I wondered what Marjorie had that I didn't have. She wasn't that pretty. I knew she was prettier than I was, but I knew she wasn't as smart. I never said much in class though, so no one knew it. When the month of May came around each school year, Marjorie was always the last one, the most special one, to crown Mary.

Mary is the patroness of the month of May. Perhaps because it is spring, and new life is beginning, and Mary is the symbol of motherhood. In our classroom we had a procession around the room every morning while we sang a hymn to Mary. A student would place a crown of flowers on the statue of Mary. We all took turns, one student for each day, but Marjorie always went last. That last place was reserved for the most special student, and it sure wasn't me.

I'd usually remember that it was my turn the night before and Mom would pull out a wire coat hanger from the closet that she twisted into a circle. I'd ask her to get me up early so I could find some flowers in the back yard.

The roses weren't in bloom--it was a little too early. Irises didn't attach very well, so I'd pick some clover, some white and some pink, and tediously tie them together, leaving a pile of broken clover stems under my swing set. My crown of flowers was definitely handmade. The sisters gave me their usual sour look, and some years the crown was too big and some years too small, when I overcompensated.

The wire stuck out in many places around the circle, and the tiny clover barely hid it. By the time I got to school, which was only one block away, it would be coming apart and I prayed it would stay together till after the morning bell.

Marjorie's crown looked like it came from a florist, which it probably did. Velvet red roses wove in and out of a sparkling wire and baby's breath peeked out to contrast with the roses. Dew hung on the roses like they had been freshly picked, and the crown was always the right size. Marjorie would walk proudly at the head of the procession around the classroom, her dainty feet in her perfectly polished Buster Brown shoes, her uniform neatly creased in all the right places, and would carefully place the crown on the head of Mary.

I could almost hear Mary saying, "Thank you, my dear. It's about time I got a crown of roses worthy of me."

And I'd sit and look at the floor and wonder why Marjorie never slipped and fell.

As I sat at meditation in the motherhouse chapel that morning, I realized that no matter how hard I tried, my crown would never be anything special. Not that I cared anymore. But I wished it had been a crown of flowers instead of gross thorns, so I could at least try to make something beautiful. I guess I still felt inadequate about my crown-making skills from grade school.

I pieced my crown together quickly over the next few weeks with sticks and thorns provided in boxes in front of the study hall. Wow, what fun. I put it in my new crown box and stuck it in my desk, embarrassed to show it to anyone, especially my parents.

The day of our profession of vows came. It was the first time I had seen my family in a year, and I was thrilled to see them. I took the stupid crown off immediately after the ceremony. Now that we had become real sisters, although we were still called junior sisters, we would get back to our visiting days once a month. It would be great to see my family every month. It had been a long year, and I hoped the worst was over with S.Regina's rigid rules and regulations.

I stuck the crown box in my drawer as we made the transition to our new dormitories in the next section of the large building.

When our first visiting day came after we had moved, I never dreamed of showing the crown again to my parents or sisters. I hoped they hadn't even noticed it at the ceremony because they'd think it was pretty stupid, too. I had practically forgotten all about it, but I noticed that Juliette brought her crown box out to show her parents.

When I walked outside with Juliette the next month, and the month after that, she brought her crown box each time. I figured she had some new relatives stopping by and she wanted to show them, so I didn't think much about it. Even though a lot of my classmates hadn't hated the crown like I did, I noticed no one else brought it out monthly to show their relatives.

Juliette ran up behind me on our morning walk after a visiting day in January.

"I have to talk to you," she exclaimed breathlessly.

"Sure. What's up?"

"I have to tell you what happened yesterday."

"Oh, did you have a nice visit?"

"Yeah, but listen to this. I'm so lucky I'm still here today."

I stopped and looked at her. "Why, what happened?"

"Well, I always take my crown box to show my parents, but I don't put the crown in it. They could care less. Me too."

She looked around to make sure no one was behind us. "I have a bottle of Jim Beam in it." She paused and looked at me.

I laughed out loud.

"So that's why you bring it out each month." It was so Juliette. I knew she missed that glass of wine at dinner that her parents had always provided.

"So, go on," I encouraged her.

"Ok, I'll give you some anytime you want, now that you know. Anyway, I put the empty Jim Beam bottle in my crown box yesterday and ran down the main stairway by Alphonse's office. I was really going fast cause I was late and I knew my parents were

148

waiting. I got down to the third-floor landing and turned the corner and there was Alphonse coming up the stairs."

"Oh, no, what did you do?" I asked, horrified. Sister Alphonse, or rather Mother Alphonse, was the superior of the whole province that stretched all the way to California. I think it skipped all the states in between Missouri and California, but at least it seemed big.

"Well, I couldn't turn around and run away so I just started praying she wouldn't say anything to me."

"Did she?"

"Well, I slowed way down and boy was I praying. If there was a prayer meter it would have shot up so high right then."

"So...go on."

"Oh, she didn't just go past me. She stopped and said, 'Praised be to you, Lord Jesus Christ,' and I kind of squeaked out, 'Now and forever, Amen.' I kept walking down the steps slowly and I thought I was home free and then I hear from behind me, 'Sister, what's your name?' "

"I swallowed hard and turned and smiled and said, 'Sister Juliette.' "

"Sister, is that your crown box?" she asked."

"I stood rooted to the spot. I couldn't move."

'Yes, sister, I mean mother," I whispered.'

'Are you going to show your crown to your parents?' she asked sweetly. I could see the little hairs sticking out of her chin and above her lip."

"I said, 'Yes, sister,' and I knew that was it. I had one more second of being a nun. A whole two and a half years totally wasted. And I had really tried hard. I knew the next sentence out of her mouth would be, 'Can I see your crown, sister?' and I'd have to open the crown box and she'd see the empty bottle and I'd go into her office and I wouldn't even have a chance to say goodbye to anybody."

"So what happened?" I asked impatiently.

"She just stood there for a few seconds like she was thinking and I was sweating and my heart was going faster and faster."

"Then she said, 'It's so nice that you are sharing your

crown with your family. Have a good visit, Sister Juliette,' and she lifted her skirts slightly as she went past me, trudging up the steps. I stood there holding the crown box so tight against me. The sweat was coming down pretty hard, and then I very quietly and carefully walked down the rest of the steps and out the front door to get my refill."

I breathed a sigh of relief. "God, you are so lucky."

"Yeah, I know. So anytime you want a drink, let me know."

I walked a few more feet in silence. "Hey, I'm just glad you're still here. That's the important thing. Maybe we should celebrate tonight after everyone goes to bed. What do you think?"

"Great." Juliette said enthusiastically. "Tonight, my place."

And we continued our walk.

Chapter 39
The Juniorate

July 1968

The July afternoon was hot, but I had pulled up a folding chair in the shade of a large oak tree on the front lawn. We had been given three days of retreat to make our final decision about continuing in the order and taking our vows. The small ceremony at the end of the retreat would be on my twentieth birthday. For the first time in two years, I had nothing to do. No classes or practicing. We still had our usual prayers, and complete silence while we meditated on our choice for the rest of our lives, but no laundry or cleaning and best of all, no instructions. I suppose if we hadn't learned all the rules by now, there was no hope at this late date.

As I sat under the oak tree and looked at the train tracks and river beyond, I wondered just how a liberal and non-traditional Catholic like me had ever ended up here in the convent--and was still here!

The sixties were a decade of extremes. There was hope with John Kennedy, Martin Luther King and Robert Kennedy, but many of the dreams of the country had died with them. The Vietnam War was heating up, and no one knew what the future would bring in terms of our young servicemen being sent to fight in a war no one wanted.

I had made this choice of convent life, but it was a choice based on my limited knowledge of the world. All I knew was what I read in books and saw on the news. I had never experienced love or suffering, a traumatic event, or real passion about something I wanted to achieve. My future had been decided based on a tiny slice of life. But it was all I had.

I thought back to the day when I met S. Rachel, the single most influential person in my decision to join. After Christmas of my junior year I was playing the piano at a chorus rehearsal one day in the high school gym. We were taking a break, and someone asked me to play "Claire de Lune" by Debussy, so I started playing the piece on the rickety old upright piano. I noticed that one of the teachers passing by had stopped to listen. I knew her. Her name was Sister Rachel, and she had been my speech teacher freshman year. I was a little scared of her because I had done so badly in speech class. My self-esteem dropped down low as I had to stand in front of a whole class and make up something to talk about. I managed to get a C for the class but hated it. I hadn't talked to Sister Rachel since. She was very young, probably 24 or 25 at the most.

She stood by the piano and when I finished, she said, "I had no idea you played so beautifully."

I said "Thanks."

"What other pieces do you play? What are your favorites?"

"I love Bach. I'm playing the Italian Concerto and a few Partitas. And I love Chopin."

She answered excitedly, "Oh, I love the Chopin Ballade Number 3. Can you play that?"

I played a few pages by memory. She put down her books on the piano and listened intently. "I try and try to play that but I never seem to get any better. You play so well."

We talked for a while about piano and then she surprised me.

"Would you help me with the music for the senior play? Not playing piano, but helping me pick out the music and be in charge of the sound?"

"Sure, I'd love to try."

I liked her that day. She treated me more like an equal than a student, and I always admired her theatre productions. Every time we met we talked more, and soon I was going to her home room after school just to talk. We talked about movies and plays, philosophy and theology. She was brilliant and witty. She thought what she wanted to think, not what others told her. She didn't seem to let being a nun get in the way of doing what she wanted.

She was my example. If I had known how unusual she was, I might not have joined. But I thought she was the future of the church. A vibrant community composed of women who could make their own decisions--and maybe someday be equal to priests.

Sister Rachel never talked about my becoming a nun. She never mentioned it at all.

152

I was thinking seriously about joining the Peace Corps, which under President Kennedy's leadership, had become a huge and successful organization. But early in 1966 my cousin got kicked out of the Peace Corps in Guatemala, for what reason I don't remember, and probably never knew, but he had plenty of terrible things to say about it. I decided then that the Peace Corps wasn't the place for me.

Sometime in that fall and winter, I began thinking about joining the convent. I was confident that the huge changes in the church would be rapid and far-reaching. I saw a woman in Sister Rachel who could be herself, independent, and not bound by all the rules. I saw her in a profession which seemed like something I wanted to do. My mother was a teacher, and I had been so profoundly influenced by Mr. Read and now Sister Rachel, that I wanted to teach others and influence people in that same way.

After a great deal of thought, I decided to join the order. I would become a teacher, and I wouldn't be bound by the rules and regulations that had so characterized the religious orders. All those rules were changing, anyway. And if they hadn't changed completely by the time I entered, I would help to make the changes.

My choice was made. I looked to a bright future full of wonderful changes, even though I was painfully aware that the convent had a long way to go. At the time, I had no idea what I would be up against.

The Novitiate was finally over. Our year of study and reflection had come to an end, and we were accepted into the order. I was twenty years old when I became a real sister, and professed my vows of poverty, chastity, and obedience at the St. Louis Cathedral. We exchanged our white veils for black ones. Even though we looked like real nuns, these were only temporary vows. We had to be in the order for six more years to be able to profess our permanent vows.

I didn't have any problems with chastity. Despite S. Beatrice's warnings about men, there simply weren't any around, except the ancient priests who came to say Mass every morning and then left as quickly as possible. I wasn't interested in men, anyway.

The vow of poverty was easy. As postulants and novices, we didn't have any possessions, but I didn't have much when I was growing up, so it was really no different. On a trip to Texas when I was twelve to visit my Uncle Jim and family, we had travelled to Monterrey, Mexico, and I had bought some beautiful glassware and some silver jewelry from Taxco. I gave it all away to my friend Carol and was able to keep all my piano music and a few records, so I was fine.

Obedience was a problem. I tended to be pretty stubborn, and did what I wanted, without anyone knowing about it. It had worked well so far. It's not that I didn't want to be a good person. It was that some of the rules were opposed to what I considered being a "good person."

But when I think back to my decision to stay and profess my vows, it all came down to two things.

The first was God. Even though I wasn't "religious" in the sense that I was outwardly pious or loved praying, the search for God meant a great deal to me.

The second reason I went ahead and professed my vows that summer was because of my friends. Those first two years were mostly a chance to make new friends. The fact that we couldn't really talk to each other stopped me from really getting to know anyone in my class, but I broke every rule I could in getting to know older friends. S. Maribeth and S. Joan had become my best friends, but now they were gone. I missed them a lot.

I got to know Pam a little better and became good friends with Juliette. She turned out to be a delightful, fun-loving girl who just wanted to have friends and be a friend. We laughed together a lot, mostly at the archaic rules. Despite all the rules about inter-class silence, I had become friends with Louise, my musical partner. I looked forward to the day where we could play together again. Since she was becoming a novice it would be a few years. But I had gotten to know a few sisters in the class ahead of me, snatches of conversations at recreation times once a month, and I looked forward to living with them. We had spent two long years without being able to talk, and now we would be with them twenty-four hours a day, building a community for the next year. It seemed ridiculous that we had wasted all that time not speaking at all.

So that was a big reason I stayed. I had friends and I didn't want to leave them. I still believed that life would get better--that S. Beatrice and S. Regina were not the future of the order. We young sisters were the future--and we would bring a lot of change to the Church.

There would be a day soon when we didn't just change our clothing habits, but the centuries-old habits of the church, and women would be equal to men.

I remember reading a fable about a frog that is thrown in boiling water and jumps out right away. But another frog is put into a pot of cold water. Instead of jumping out, the frog sits in the water as it's heated up slowly and dies. I think I was that frog. I didn't notice that I was dying inside--and I stayed--and stayed. Way too long.

I had chosen this life and was determined to be successful at it. All the while, the water was heating up, and still this frog didn't jump out. I didn't realize at the time how difficult--no, impossible--it would be for the church to change.

Sisters Beatrice and Regina were relics of the past, and now I hoped I'd have a lot of liberal-minded and forward-thinking people in charge of our development as sisters.

Chapter 40
The River

I was thrilled to be so close to the river when I entered the convent, but for the first two years I lived on the opposite side of the building and saw the river only on walks around the building. I would peek through the trees on the front lawn and see glimpses, and I saw it that Christmas Eve when Elena and I went out on the roof, but most of the time it was tantalizingly out-of-reach.

After two long years, moving into the juniorate meant that I got to change dorms and for the first time, was in a small dorm overlooking the Mississippi River. It was on the fourth floor of the motherhouse, and I could sit on my bed--I had a window again-- and look at the river.

If I had any minutes of free time during the day I would look out the window to the green lawns stretching to the railroad tracks and beyond that, the river. At night I could see the few lights of the city and the sulfur plant, and I could see the twinkling lights of the barges and riverboats as they slipped through the velvety night, behind dark trees, and reappeared further downriver. The chains clanking on the barges, and the churning of the motors as they pushed against the strong current put me to sleep at night.

I set my alarm clock twenty minutes early, yes, that early, so I could sit cross-legged on my bed and watch the sunrise over the river. Sometimes the clouds were orange-red and gold from the rising sun, and at other times the sun was a white ball reflecting silver on the rippling water. I had very little time during the day, so early morning and late at night were my special times to watch the Mississippi's many moods.

"I think the river is a strong brown god." T.S. Eliot begins one of his most famous poems with that beautiful line. Growing up in St. Louis meant growing up with rivers. Not just the wide Missouri River, but also the mighty Mississippi.

They were both rivers of legend, from the Cahokia Indians who settled a short distance from them, to the stories of Mark Twain, the journeys of Lewis and Clark, and the poetry of T.S. Eliot.

I remember standing at the bottom of the cobblestones

156

leading down to the St. Louis riverfront on the Mississippi. I was very small and then taller through successive years, but the river always remained the same, swirling brown past my feet and lapping on the dusty gray cobblestones. It was always exciting to watch. There were barges going up and down, car and train traffic on the Eads Bridge, and the smoky bluffs far across the river in Illinois.

My grandmother's brother had died during the construction of the Eads Bridge in the 1860's. I think he fell from it. I always thought about him when I saw the bridge and wondered what his life might have been like if he had lived.

We never swam in the river. It was too strong and powerful. The Missouri River joined the Mississippi north of St. Louis, and if the Mississippi was the "old man" of rivers, then the Missouri was an unruly teenager. Its currents flowed more swiftly and wildly, and it had very few places to just stand and watch from its banks. It dug into forests and bluffs. Trees would hang over its edges for years until they'd finally fall in the river and be swept downstream.

My friend Donna and I would go downtown every Saturday when we were juniors and seniors in high school. The river became part of the ritual. We'd walk down to the riverfront, past the paved streets and on to the old cobblestone streets of a century past. We'd walk past the new arch to check on how far the construction had gotten. Donna and I laughed at the huge stainless-steel arch. We thought the millions of dollars would be better spent on education or helping the poor.

I'm glad to admit we were wrong. The arch became the symbol of the city and probably brought more revenue than anything else in its history. We watched its long process of construction, from the museum underneath to the huge supports for the legs. We could see the legs being built, one piece at a time, and the cranes and supports got higher and higher until the very last piece was set in place with the hope that it would fit perfectly.

My mother's fourth grade class watched the last section being put in the arch on the classroom TV. My mom was explaining how difficult it was to get the measurements perfect and how they hoped the top section would fit. A little boy raised his

157

hand and said, "Why didn't they just start at the top?" I don't think my mom had an answer for that, but we certainly laughed about it around the dinner table.

Donna and I would walk past the arch construction and get on the Admiral, an old stainless-steel riverboat whose heyday had been in the 1930's. It had fallen into disrepair and disinterest by the sixties, but drunks and a few bored teenagers joined a small stream of tourists waiting in line for each river excursion. They would ooh and aah about the river all the way downstream and back up again. Donna and I were cooler than that. We sat looking bored with our Cokes and popcorn and talked about important things. We talked about movies, especially the newly released "Lawrence of Arabia," our teachers at school, and joked about what we'd do with our lives.

But the only thing I remember from all those conversations is the river and its power. I remember watching the broken logs and debris that swirled like matchsticks, bobbing and being pulled underneath the water till they reappeared further downstream. I was careful not to seem like a tourist, but deep inside I was and always would be gawking inwardly at the Mississippi's tremendous power and beauty.

The river had always been a part of my life, but I never experienced its many moods and colors like I did that summer. I felt sick when we moved that fall into our regular dorms on the other side of the building and tan hospital curtains surrounded me on all four sides. I missed most the sounds in the dark, late at night, of the barges and riverboats and the long whistle of the train going by. It was hard to fall asleep entombed in the silence of those heavy curtains.

Even though the river had been given and then taken away so quickly, there were lots of other perks of becoming a junior sister. One was that S. Regina was no longer in charge of us. I felt sorry for my friend Louise being in the novitiate, but I was free. Sister Rose was our juniorate mistress. She was in her fifties and had a more casual attitude about our development. After all, we had already been "developed" for two years, and I guess we were turning into the very proper "picture" of what nuns should look like. As long as we didn't commit any mortal sins or promote

158

atheism, she didn't seem to care very much. That was a welcome change for me.

The other perk was that the seniors and juniors were combined into one big group. We hadn't built much of a community in our group of twenty-eight in those first two years because of the time restrictions, the prayers and the constant fear of particular friendships.

There were a lot of adjustments in the juniorate. Because we had a whole new group of friends to choose from, best friends went by the wayside, and new friendships were formed. People we had forbidden to speak with, we were now encouraged to become friends with. It was like the section of forbidden chocolates in the candy store was now available.

Another exciting and long-awaited event took place. The centuries-old serge habits were thrown out and we got to wear a blue skirt, white blouse, and a simple black veil. My hair was free, at least in the front! I had gotten rid of the habit, the novitiate, and S. Regina in the space of a few short months. I almost felt like a human again, instead of some dressed-up symbol of oppression. Even more than the habit's unflattering feminine-cancelling ability, and its silent bow to the traditions of centuries past, it was also just plain hot. I was thrilled I would never have to go through another summer without air conditioning and with the weight of the scratchy habit. Many of the older sisters chose to keep the old habit. But I didn't know of anyone under fifty who didn't welcome the change. It was so wonderful to be released from our "fabric prison."

I got to know a senior named Patrice. She was thin and wiry with black hair. She thought of herself as an artist, a philosopher, a person who was special and above everyone else. I became good friends with her. I liked her because she thought she was special, and I had just enough of the snob in me that I was attracted to her intelligence. We talked a lot about the future of our lives and where the church was heading in terms of reforms.

We had an extra heavy load of classes because we had "wasted" a whole academic year in the novitiate learning to be nuns. As upper classmen we had to take heavy college schedules to get our degrees and teaching credentials in three years instead of four.

I had new friends, new classes, a new superior that didn't seem to care much about the rules, a new habit, and I was only two years away from graduating, getting my degree, and becoming a teacher. The juniorate was so much better than the novitiate that I was happy I had decided to go on. Any doubts I had were swept away with the joy of taking classes and being a real college student again.

Chapter 41
Pianos and Popcorn

After the frustration and humiliation of my "concert" with Louise, I alternated between feeling very depressed about playing the piano and determined to be the very best I could--mostly to show S. Regina that she was wrong.

Louise's experience of the recital was very different. Everyone in her class enjoyed it, complimented her on her playing, and hoped we would play again. Sister Beatrice and S. Susan liked it a lot, she said.

I couldn't tell Louise what had happened. I was still angry about it, and I didn't have more than a few minutes to talk to her anyway--she was still in the novitiate. I did tell her our practices were over and there would be no more concerts. I felt completely alone in my anger and frustration.

Sister Verene called me into her office in October. "There's a Young Artists Competition sponsored by the St. Louis Symphony in January. I think you should try out for it. Anyway, don't decide now. Just keep practicing the Beethoven's 4th Concerto, and we'll talk soon. Think about it."

I was thrilled that S. Verene thought I was good enough to participate in the competition, but I wondered how those two attitudes could live side-by-side in this same building. The attitude from S. Regina that hated my performance, basically said I had no humility and that I was a show-off and a disgrace--and this other attitude which celebrated and appreciated my talent.

Besides being angry and confused, I was afraid because I simply didn't know if I was good enough.

There were only two music majors in my class. That wasn't much of a cross-section. My old piano teacher in grade school and high school had gone to Juilliard, but I never even knew that till my senior year. She suggested then that I apply for Juilliard, but it was too late as I had already decided to join the convent and had given up a few scholarships to Washington University and St. Louis University. I couldn't go to Juilliard anyway. My parents would never be able to afford it.

I had no idea how well I would do in the competition or

even how I compared to other pianists my age.

S. Verene signed me up after I agreed, and I practiced hours every day perfecting Beethoven's Fourth Piano Concerto. It would be incredible to play it with a real orchestra if I ever got that far. Sister Verene walked into the practice room one day. It was the only practice room with a grand piano, and I was thrilled to be able to use it.

"Sorry to interrupt you, but come on over here, please."

I hoped I wasn't in trouble with S. Verene! I really liked her and couldn't imagine what I had done wrong. She had never corrected me for anything before. I walked over to where she was standing next to a six-foot potted plant in the corner.

"Look at the size of those new leaves. They're almost twice the size of the old ones. I think it's ever since you started practicing in here. Do you think it responds to the vibrations?"

At first I thought she was crazy. But I looked at the leaves, and there was an obvious difference. And I was the only person practicing in the room.

"I don't know," I said honestly, smiling to myself.

"Well, I just don't know what else it could be. Go ahead, keep practicing. I just wanted to show you this." She smiled.

I was at least doing some good with all my hard work. Look at that, S. Regina!

Christmas came and I was increasingly nervous about the competition. But I was getting about as good as I could get. I'd be ready in a month, even though my mouth got dry and my stomach churned at the thought.

One evening we made popcorn during our recreation hour. That was quite a treat. Not everybody wanted some, but a small group of us stood around the electric popcorn popper. I was closest to it, talking to Juliette. Someone turned quickly and tripped on the cord. The two-quart popper flew off the table. Without thinking, I reached out and grabbed it with both my hands, then as the pain hit, I dropped it.

I burned both my hands badly. Everyone helped when they saw what had happened, got cold water to soak them, and butter to put on them later, but the damage was done.

The pain was intense. I had a new compassion for burn

victims. The pain they must go through! And I had only burned my hands!

A few minutes later, as I went upstairs and S. Rose assessed the damage, I suddenly realized that I could never play in the competition. I spent a few sleepless nights in our infirmary, but my hands took months to heal.

Sister Verene was very disappointed, and I was disappointed--and relieved at the same time. I would never know how I would have done--or if I had a chance of winning.

I played the Beethoven piano concerto for my senior recital, but always wondered what might have happened if I had competed.

Would I have won, left the convent and become a concert pianist? Would I have lost and been humiliated by my performance? I always wondered what my life would have been like without the popcorn.

Chapter 42
The Real Silent Night

One of our chores as a junior sister was to visit the elderly nuns in our infirmary. The infirmary was on the fourth floor of the motherhouse, above the novitiate. Some of my classmates were good at visiting. Jan could talk to anyone, and her light chatter made the older nuns look up and smile. I really didn't know what to say to them. I was too shy to ask many questions. I didn't know which sisters were mentally alert or who had dementia. I felt, as young people often do, very self-conscious around the elderly.

I had never met my German grandmother. She had emigrated with my grandfather Gustave but missed her family back in Germany and had a difficult time learning English, so they divorced and she moved back. She lived in Hamburg until she died in the sixties. My grandfather Gustave, who had settled in St. Louis, was a strict and mean man who for some reason loved my sister Jane the most of his three grandchildren. Carol and I were ignored. My grandfather and father hadn't spoken in many years, because of some forgotten argument that my grandfather held onto. My mother finally urged my father to call him, and they talked again and met and reconnected after forty years. Unfortunately, my grandfather died soon after that. What a lot of wasted years.

I remember my Irish grandmother more, bustling around her large home in Maplewood, a suburb of St. Louis. She had raised seven children and had many, many grandchildren, but I remember the old house much more than I remember her.

The polished wooden bannisters and the staircase to the second floor are etched in my memory. I spent hours sitting on the stairs and the landing reading a book. I always brought a book. It was easier to read than to talk. I remember running out on the large wooden porch, the grey boards creaking as I walked over to the porch swing. The dining room had beautiful blue patterned plates all around the ceiling, and a huge mahogany table that I sat under while I played with my toys. I loved playing with my cousin Tommy. He was closest in age to me and had recently lost his father.

Every summer, the back yard had tomatoes planted in the

garden, a favorite pastime of my Irish grandfather, and I remember the wooden door to the cellar, and him lifting it up carefully, and us walking hand in hand down the cellar steps. The walls were cold and damp and the cellar was dark.

Thomas Kelly was my favorite grandparent. I remember him holding me in his arms when I was about three or four, as we stood by the train tracks and counted the cars on the freight train. One time we counted over a hundred cars. He was a train man his whole life. He worked for the Missouri-Pacific Railroad and was the sweetest and kindest man I've ever known. After my grandmother died, he came to live with us for a few months, and I liked him.

I was too shy to talk to him and I don't remember much except that he went into a nursing home soon after. Many years after he died, I dreamt we were all sitting around in a circle and I realized he was sitting next to me. I tried to talk to him in the dream, and he turned to me but couldn't speak.

When it came to visiting with the elderly sisters in the infirmary, I never knew what to say. One afternoon I was sitting with a sister in her room--she seemed like she was over a hundred years old--wishing my time was up and I could leave, when I mentioned that I was a musician.

"Have you ever heard of the name Gruber?" she asked.

"No, not really." I answered. We were a German order, and there were so many German names no one could keep track of them all.

She said, "My great-grandfather was the musician, Franz Gruber, who wrote "Silent Night." Suddenly visiting this old nun seemed pretty interesting. I asked her all about her great-grandfather, what stories he had told her, and what she remembered about him.

She told me the story of how the organ broke on Christmas Eve and how he wrote a song for Midnight Mass with the lyrics that the parish priest had given him. It was a simple piece for voice and guitar, and he sang it that evening at the little church where he was the music director. That piece was "Silent Night." I had heard the story before but this time I knew it was true. She probably heard it directly from her grandfather. Our connection was made through the wonderful gift of music.

There was no reason not to believe her, but it wasn't till recently that I could check out Ancestry on the internet and found that it was true--her age and his lifespan made the timeline possible.

I went every Thursday afternoon to visit her for a few months, until she became very ill and I couldn't see her anymore. I remember her funeral mass in our chapel. Funerals in the Catholic liturgy were really occasions for joy since the person has hopefully gone to heaven and was with God. In the convent it was even a more joyous celebration, because we were living our whole lives for Christ and being with him was our ultimate goal.

But my heart couldn't find any joy in that day. I would miss her.

And I've always felt a special connection with that piece of music. Most things from two hundred years ago are long forgotten; important political pronouncements, wars, literature of the time seems dated, even portraits of famous people have grown darker and forgotten.

But music seems to retain its youth and vibrancy, and listening to "Silent Night," it sounds as beautiful and fresh as it must have sounded that Christmas two hundred years ago. When I listen to it, it reminds me of the elderly sister, but even more, it reminds me of the power of music to connect us not only across our man-made borders, but even across the centuries.

Chapter 43
Alcoholics Anonymous

Gluttony, one of the seven deadly sins, wasn't a problem for me. I was very thin in the convent, thinner than I've ever been since then. The food we were served was excellent, made with care by the sisters in the Big Kitchen. What a job that must have been. Rising before anyone else, making pots of scrambled eggs, oatmeal, and then lunches and dinners for the whole motherhouse, including the postulants, novices, faculty, administrators, and the nuns in the infirmary. What a life. I couldn't even imagine it.

Catholics are known for having feast days for saints. There are so many saints they can't fit onto a calendar. They have to pile them up, maybe three or four on each day of the year. We couldn't possibly celebrate all the feast days, just the big ones. And we'd always have wine for feast days.

I had never had any wine growing up like Juliette. My dad liked to drink Cokes, and he would have a Falstaff beer in the refrigerator for six months before he got around to drinking it. My mom didn't drink at all. They weren't against it; they just didn't like to drink.

When I was a junior sister, every so often I had cart duty, the job of bringing the carts of food from the Big Kitchen to our dining room at the other end of the motherhouse. After the meal another junior sister and I would return the cart and help the kitchen nuns with washing and drying the big pots and pans.

It took about fifteen minutes to roll the cart from one end of the building to the other. The juniorate was at the far end of the complex of buildings, and the big kitchen was in the main section of the motherhouse.

On a feast day, everyone had a glass of wine in celebration, but most of the nuns didn't drink, so on the return trip at least half of the glasses hadn't been touched. No one said we couldn't drink them, so Sister Frances and I had a few sips on the way back. The next feast day we had a few more, and then it became a regular ritual--we were big on rituals in the convent.

We did have a variety of different wines each feast day, but I had no idea what they were. I knew they were red, white, or something in-between. That was the extent of my knowledge. And I had some of Juliette's Jim Beam every so often, but it tasted horrible. I didn't know how she could drink it! What we salvaged from the dinner carts, though, was certainly better than the sacramental wine we tasted on holy days when we received the Body and Blood of Jesus at communion.

I've read what AA has to say about drinking alone, and many other tell-tale signs of alcoholism. Drinking from the dinner cart probably wouldn't be listed, although it could have been. But all too soon, after six months of waiting anxiously for those glorious feast days, I was off cart duty and on to some other boring cleaning chore. Whatever it was, it wasn't nearly as refreshing--or as much fun.

Chapter 44
The Pieta Goes Missing

I was a junior sister, so I had more freedom. Novices, with their white veils, were easy to spot and get in trouble, but wearing a black veil helped me blend in, since all the real sisters wore black veils. Even Pam was getting better at being inconspicuous--well, not much--although she still managed to attract trouble every week or so. We had already professed our vows as sisters, so the superiors in the juniorate didn't have all that much to do except keep us in line--studying and doing our chores. Following the rules took a lot less time than learning about them.

One evening, I went over to Sister Barbara's office. She was chair of the English department; I was an English major, as well as music, and we had become friends after I took a few of her classes. We got to talking, and she got some extra cokes out of a cooler in her office, and we talked for hours.

Barbara was in her early thirties and interesting. She had her PhD in English Literature and was an excellent teacher.

We talked about books and school and life till after midnight. I counted twelve chimes from the grandfather clock on the floor below, then one for 12:30, and another single one for one o'clock. We were in the college part of the motherhouse, completely empty at night. I would have gotten in trouble if anyone had noticed I wasn't in the dorm at that time, but Sister Barbara had enough clout to get me out of trouble.

The postulants were asleep a few floors above us, but we were the only ones on the second floor. Then we heard it. The tinny doorbell at the main entrance on the main floor.

"Is that the doorbell?" she looked worried when she heard the sound. It was one in the morning!

"I don't know. It's after midnight. Who could be ringing the doorbell at this time of night?"

We looked at each other. Maybe it would stop. Nobody was going to answer the door at one am. Then the knocking started, and the doorbell again.

Sister Beatrice had installed a fear of men lurking everywhere, in the basement showers especially. That was the first thing I thought of. Someone had come to rob the convent. Or assault us! It didn't occur to me at that moment that "lurking men" or "robbers" probably wouldn't ring the doorbell!

The tinny bell rang and rang. Barbara stood up. "I'm going down. Come with me!"

She grabbed my arm. I didn't want to go--the same feeling as having a tooth pulled--but I didn't want her to go alone either, so I followed her down the two flights of stairs. We stood at the dark wooden door.

She yelled, "Who is it? What do you want?"

"Lemay police, ma'am. We'd like to talk to you."

I peered through the fuzzy stained glass at the side of the door and could see the red flashing lights of the patrol car. I nodded to her. It really was the police.

Barbara unlocked a few locks and opened the door an inch.

"Sorry to bother you," said a heavyset policeman. A younger, slimmer version of him stood by his side.

"We were investigating a home in the area, and we found hundreds of large religious statues in the garage. We were wondering if you were missing any?"

Barbara usually wasn't speechless, and I had never heard her stutter. She was always at ease in every situation.

"Uh, ...uh..., I don't think we're missing any."

The larger policeman handed her a card.

"Well, ma'am, I mean sister, if you're missing any in the next few days, call this number and let us know."

The other policeman said, "They really are very large statues--life size ones--and we couldn't think of any other place they would have come from."

Barbara found her teacher voice. "I certainly will check. Thank you." And she closed the door politely.

Barbara put her finger on her lips. We waited until the patrol car pulled away, then burst out laughing. We tried to stop, but it was hard. Just the thought of some man driving a truck, coming up to the front entrance, somehow making it into the building and taking all our statues was ridiculous.

We did have a lot of statues, though. Statues of Mary, Mary with Joseph, Jesus and various saints scattered around alcoves,

170

where we could kneel and get in an extra prayer and light a candle if we felt like it. I don't remember ever feeling like it.

For the next week I looked at statues. I hadn't really noticed them before. They were all still there, as far as I could tell. No empty alcoves or spaces where a statue might have been. I took my finger and touched them and tried to figure out what they were made of. Some might have been marble, I guess, but most seemed to be plaster with really bad paint jobs.

We never called back the Lemay police, and to this day, I wonder why the strange man had a garage full of life size religious statues--and where he had gotten them.

Chapter 45
The Moon

It would be hard to pick the most frustrating event of my convent years--there are so many to choose from--but one of them happened on July 20, 1969, the night of the first moon landing. Ever since President Kennedy had announced that we would have a man on the moon by the end of the decade, space travel had become a national obsession. The country was brought together by this dream of a mission to the moon, and the astronauts were national heroes. The United States wanted to reach the moon ahead of the Russians, and the space race captured the imagination of the whole country.

I had always been fascinated by the space program. My uncle was an engineer for NASA and worked at Cape Canaveral. I was proud of his role, however small, in the space program. We waited with the whole world as the mission to the moon took off from the Cape and hurled through space toward its destination.

The evening was hot and sticky since it was the middle of summer. We were all packed in the recreation room in the basement of the motherhouse with only one TV set, to watch the historic event. After the lunar module landed on the surface, there were still many hours of preparation before they could take their first step. The audio and video were coming through beautifully, and we sat glued to the television, just like the rest of the world.

What an incredible event was unfolding before our eyes. We were about to see the first person in all of history step out onto another world.

The clock chimed nine times. Sister Rose, our junior mistress, got up, quickly walked over to the television set, and clicked it off.

Everyone in the room stared at her. She said quickly, "Sisters, it's time to go to bed. Just because there's a TV program on you want to watch is no excuse for breaking the rules." And she turned and walked out of the room.

I thought it was a joke at first. She was coming back in the room any second, and would say, "I'm just kidding" and turn the set back on. Only she didn't. A few minutes passed, and a few

172

obedient sisters got up and left the room. Sister Rose walked in again and said more insistently, "It's time for bed, sisters," and walked out of the room into her office. I sat there, unbelieving. She wasn't joking and she wasn't coming back.

Some of my classmates looked a little disappointed, and some shrugged their shoulders, but most of them got up and walked out of the room to get ready for bed. I sat rooted to my seat. I don't think I had ever been so angry.

I finally gave up and went to the big chapel, hoping to meet up with Louise, who was still a novice. We met often in the chapel at night and whispered about what was going on in our lives. Louise was in the choir loft when I got there. They couldn't watch the moon landing either. S. Regina had been replaced but even the new novice mistress wouldn't have permitted it.

"Let's go up on the roof," Louise whispered. "At least we can see the moon out there."

"Ok," I answered. I was ready to call my parents and have them come and get me, but I couldn't get to a telephone. The roof was about the best we could do.

We grabbed a flashlight, climbed up the wide main stairs to the fourth floor, went through a small door into the attic, and pushed open the little door and crawled out on the roof.

The gray tiles of the roof were warm from the summer heat. We put a brick in the door to hold it open and crawled out. The stars hung low in the sky and the moon, the bright moon, was over the Mississippi River. The river was a dark smudge on the horizon, with a few barge lights blinking on and off. The big oak trees around the motherhouse were still in the hot and humid night.

Louise and I lay down on the roof, partly because it was a little scary to stand up on it, and partly to see the moon better.

At that moment, Armstrong was preparing to take his first step, the "small step for man, the giant step for mankind." And we were seeing as much as we were going to see. We knew that billions of people all over the world were glued to their TV sets, probably everyone except us. I thought of the people in Europe and Russia and Africa who were watching. And we had a perfectly good TV just a few floors beneath us. And unable to watch all because of some stupid rule and some stupid person who thought it was more important to go to bed than to watch the moon landing.

I was ready to leave the convent that night. I don't know how ready Louise was, but she was close. We all left eventually.

In 1989, the 20th anniversary of the moon landing, one of the TV stations in Los Angeles ran the complete broadcast of the landing. I said angrily to my husband Don, "I'm going to sit down and watch the whole thing, and no one's going to stop me."

"Sure, watch the whole thing. That's fine." He was surprised at my anger. He was in the army at the time and wasn't able to watch it either.

I watched the whole broadcast from beginning to end. I felt that I had missed one of the most important moments of my lifetime. There would never be a first like that again. The first time anyone had ever set foot on another object in space. And that moment brought everyone in the world together. In peace, not fighting each other. Together in hope for a shared future. And I missed it because of some stupid rule.

The water around the frog was getting hotter and hotter, and even though it hadn't reached the point where the frog was dying, it got awfully close that hot summer night. Even though I didn't leave that night, I never forgot what I had missed.

Chapter 46
Fire and Brimstone

I was sitting in the library one afternoon, reading my American Literature textbook. I looked out the window to my right, the oak trees on the front lawn beautiful in the sunlight. I missed my oak tree in front of my house.

I hadn't even thought of it for three years, but it had marked all the seasons of my life. I had watched its black branches like a faded photograph in the swirling snow. In the spring, tiny dots of green gradually spread over all the branches. It was like a sculpture I had seen once, black metal coiled in the shape of a tree, with green glass jewels dotting the metal. By this time, the green covered the whole tree like velvet. And I always missed the fall. That was the best time. I'd collect acorns and watch as the tree turned golden and red. Mom and I would rake the leaves, smelling the wood smoke from fireplaces in the brisk fall air.

Enough of daydreaming--or meditation as I liked to call it. I glanced back to the book I was reading. We had to read the sermons of Jonathan Edwards, a preacher from the 1700's. One of his sermons was called," Sinners in the Hands of an Angry God." He talked a lot about hell and suffering and fire and brimstone. Thank God we had a more modern view of God, that he was kind and compassionate, although I did believe that people still went to hell. What it was like, I had no idea. I often thought that people made their own hells, and I wondered how compassionate God could really be if he made people suffer for all eternity. Couldn't they be given another chance? That seemed more compassionate than eternal flames. I glanced out the window again. To my left, marring the view of the trees, was the sulfur factory.

It was located on the property next to the motherhouse and every time the wind came from the north, we would see a yellow haze over the front lawns and the air would smell like rotten eggs.

It was busy today, the smokestack belching yellow smoke which often blanketed our motherhouse with the disgusting smell. A huge mountain of yellow stuff lay piled up around the factory, but for all those years I never knew what the factory did, if they produced it or processed it, or even what it was used for.

I don't think any of us gave it a second thought back in the sixties, but now people are very concerned about what they were exposed to in their childhood and youth. Who knows what illnesses I have, or will have, because of breathing sulfuric acid a few times a week for four years?

Fire is supposed to be the main ingredient of hell. I hadn't thought about the brimstone till that morning as I read Edward's sermon. Brimstone was sulfur.

We had our own little hell right next to us. Maybe it was a reminder to keep our vows and try to be very good nuns. The haze wasn't too bad most days, but we were often reminded of just how close the factory was to us.

Over the years, when I would see the yellow haze from the factory, I would wonder about the theological implications of the factory. Were we being punished in some biblical sense? Maybe God really didn't like nuns?

I never came to any conclusion about the sulfur factory, but I can attest from my own personal experience that it would be a great addition to hell along with the fire. And combined with St. Louis humidity and heat during the summer, it was often almost unbearable.

The motherhouse is still there on the banks of the river. I wonder if the sulfur factory is still there too. Perhaps it got relocated to lower regions, where it would be put to even better use.

Chapter 47
Particular Friendships--Part 2

By the time I was a senior, I had forgotten all about my instructions about close friendships from Sister Beatrice and S. Regina. I was trying to get good grades, graduate, get ready for practice teaching, and then move out of the motherhouse to my new mission, wherever that would be.

I took one last Scripture class along with my other classes. We all got a minor in theology, and I really liked my teacher, Sister Frances. She was only five to eight years older than us, had just gotten her PhD from a prestigious Catholic university, was fun and always smiling. She had a very liberal attitude and seemed horrified at the conservative direction the church was taking.

We got to talking one afternoon after class--I barely made it back in time for prayers. After that, we talked regularly, and I would go over to her office often in the afternoon after my cleaning chores.

One day after class, she asked me to pray later in the evening in her office. I said, "Sure," and assumed it was some kind of prayer group, as if we didn't pray enough. After all, she had just been promoted to the chair of the theology department. But often a "prayer group" was just a code word for a group of us getting together and chatting.

When I arrived, there was no one else in her office. We could have just talked--she didn't need to tell me it was a prayer session.

Then she said, "Let's go to an empty classroom." I walked after her, a little confused, and we went in one of the old classrooms on the third floor. She closed the door and pulled two chairs over by the window. The lights were off, but there were lights from the sulfur factory and spotlights high on the building.

We prayed for a while, asking God for blessings and talked a little about our hopes and dreams for the future.

She reached over to me and took my hand.

"You're so talented. I'm so glad I got to know you." And then she reached up and touched my face. I pulled back, but not very far.

"It's okay. God meant for us to love each other. All these restrictions about friendship are meaningless. You're a beautiful person and you deserve love."

She moved closer to me and touched my face again gently. "I really like you a lot." She kept moving closer.

I sat frozen, not quite sure what to do. I looked at my watch, barely able to make out the time, and told her I should probably leave.

"I hope you're okay with this, Susan? I hope you don't think anything's wrong with it. I would really like to be your friend. A really good friend. Do you want that too?"

"I'm not sure," I replied quickly. "I just really should go."

I walked quickly back through the deserted corridor. I was confused--torn with different emotions. It was wonderful to be liked and appreciated. Someone thought I was special. After all the humiliations and tearing down of the past three years, to have someone say such nice things was like finding water in the desert.

But I wasn't sure what she wanted. I knew we had to avoid those particular friendships, but what were they exactly? Did they involve touching or kissing or what? Or more than that? I wasn't sure. I disagreed with almost everything we had ever learned from the convent and church. Maybe the Catholic church was wrong about that too. I was almost sure it was. But it was so ingrained in me to think of homosexuality as a sin that I couldn't think anything else at the moment.

She was a teacher, and head of a department in the college, and I didn't want to make her angry. My grade might depend on my response. It was a bad position to be in.

I liked her a lot, but I didn't love her, or at least what I thought love was supposed to be. She was an amazing person and I wanted to be friends with her, but I wasn't ready for anything else. I was so confused by the time I got back to my dorm, I lay awake for hours trying to figure out what to do. But I knew I should do something. I couldn't ignore her for the rest of the semester. Or perhaps I could. That would be the coward's way out, but I didn't know what else to do. I ended up taking the cowards' way out.

178

Chapter 48
The Tunnel

We heard a lot at instructions about our potential suffering as Christians, but I never knew how removed I was from any actual suffering until October of my senior year. I didn't want to be living in that "ivory tower" that was the symbol of privilege and seclusion from the real world. I wanted to help people. Hopefully I would help students someday by teaching them, but all I had done so far was selfishly amass large amounts of knowledge that didn't seem to have any practical use.

One evening during dinner, I heard about an accident down past our front lawn toward the river. There were the train tracks and beyond that, large water retention areas and then the river.

A man had fallen in a huge pipe by the river--someone mentioned it at dinner. I remember thinking "poor man, I hope he's alright" and then went on eating. Dinner consisted of the usual stilted conversation, especially at Sister Rose's table. There was cleaning to be done after dinner, and a trip to the big kitchen. There were a lot of people gathered out front by this time. I thought it silly to be outside watching like a crowd of animals, gawking at the misfortune of another.

I stayed and worked--up and down the length of the hall until we were so tired it was all we could do to finish, hang up the mops, and run outside for some fresh air. The grounds were strangely silent, the weather hot and cloying. The September evening had a slight, warm breeze. The white sun would be down in a few hours. The sky was getting darker, but we decided to have one quick walk around the building and then go in. As soon as we came around the corner of the building, I could see the fire engines, the mad lights spinning wildly.

And down the lawn towards the river were all the people standing and talking like it was the line for the evening show.

I stopped and asked someone what was happening.

"He's still in there. His back might be broken so they can't do anything till a doctor comes."

"But it's been almost two hours."

"I know. They can't seem to find a doctor who will come

and climb through all those pipes. We're lucky we have the ambulance. They had to decide if they could get it without permission. They had to decide if it was on our property. All that took time."

I stood there silently. I wanted to leave--it was against my principles to stand there gaping like a curious child at such a tragedy, the news of the neighborhood. The person next to me moved down the hill to find someone to talk to. I went with her.

The closer I got, the more I heard what had happened. The man, a soldier, had just returned from Vietnam, and the large pipes that carried the water down to the Mississippi River had been redone. He was crawling through with a cousin, for fun, like they used to do when they were teenagers, and he didn't know the pipe had been rerouted and now dropped off 30 feet. He had fallen and there was no way out but to pull him up. It was darker now. A car drove up and a stocky sober faced doctor hurried out and walked quickly over to the scene of the accident.

I tried to imagine the soldier's feelings--the horrific pain. The darkness--looking for oneself and seeing nothing but the flashing hideous colors that come to the eyes when there is total blackness. The feel of fear--cold dead concrete--a living tomb with walls that didn't close but that tunneled deep for miles--and echoed every uncaring sound of the swirling river and dark musky earth.

The doctor went down. People were getting restless, some started up the hill. The sun had gone down and the trees were shadows pasted on the grey sky.

Suddenly I heard it. It was not human; it was the insane, low sobbing moan--pain that no one could endure. It cried through the tunnels and hung in the dead air for an eternity of seconds.

A deathly quiet came over everyone. Some stood frozen-- tears came to my eyes, as a reflex. I had never heard a cry like that before. I had only read newspaper headlines about people's sufferings. Nothing like this had ever penetrated my life. I had lived in an insulated box my entire life. My childhood was happy, with no traumatic experiences, and I enjoyed a privileged life in the convent where I got free meals and housing and education. All I had to do was study, pray, and do a few chores. I had no idea what life was like.

He lived, I heard later, but he was paralyzed from the waist down. What a price to pay for a little adventure. After all he had been through in the war, he didn't deserve any more pain. And I realized there was so much pain in the world that I had never seen or experienced. I thanked God for that but wondered how I could ever help anyone who was suffering.

My tears were not for that man, but for all the pain in the world that I had never cared about--never even imagined. It became real. As real as it could be for someone who had never really experienced pain or suffering.

Chapter 49
Particular friendships--Part 3

I avoided Sister Frances. I only had a few more months of her class. She followed me out of class one day. "I hope you aren't upset with our conversation the other night, Susan" She looked around to make sure no one was around. "We have such archaic ideas about love and friendship in this order. God wants us to love each other. I would really like to show you what that means to me. We can talk about it more this evening. Why don't you come up to my office?"

I gave her a quick excuse about being busy with an English paper that was due the next day. After that, she didn't ask me anymore. We were always polite to each other, but I left class quickly and always made sure someone was with me.

I had a lot of friendships in the convent, but I hadn't learned much more about sex in the three years of college. My knowledge was very much like the newspapers we read every day. Completely missing!

One evening a few weeks later I asked Maureen where Laura was. We needed to finish an English project together.

"Oh, she went to talk to Sister Frances."

I watched for Laura, but she never came back, and later that night I walked by her dorm area on the way to bed. She wasn't there. I had my suspicions but couldn't imagine that Frances was doing the same thing with another student.

I said nothing. Who would I tell, and what would I say?

One evening Maureen and I were studying together for a math test. My last math class forever, I hoped! We got to talking, and Maureen said,

"I'm kind of worried about Laura."

"What do you mean?"

"She's been crying every night in the dorm. It's when she comes back from seeing Sister Frances."

I was kind of slow with the "particular friendship thing," but the alarm bells went off in my mind right away. I knew exactly what was happening.

I saw it happen for months. Frances looked through me

like I didn't exist. Laura was her favorite. And then it was over. Mary Louise started going over to Frances' office. A lot. In the evenings. And getting back very late.

We were about to go out to our practice teaching assignments, and I pushed any thoughts about "particular friendships" to the back of my mind.

The present was filled with last-minute papers, excitement about out assignments, exams, and finally the day came when two sisters drove down from Quincy, Illinois, to pick up Judith and me for our six weeks of practice teaching. I got a "B" in Frances' theology class. I didn't argue with the grade.

I had no words fat that time for what had happened. It wasn't till much later that I realized what Frances was--a predator. She was a charming person who had power over us and was using it for her advantage. I was so glad I wasn't part of the group of sisters who were "used" by her. I initially felt bad when I turned down her interest, only to realize that she had no interest in me, or any of us.

Chapter 50
Practice Teaching

June 1970

I woke up slowly in a small retreat house overlooking the Mississippi River. The thin sheet barely touched my body. The brightness filled my closed eyes, the sunlight and shadow flickering as the tree branches outside the window swayed in the breeze. I lay in bed in my own room, alone, and felt like I was floating. I opened my eyes slowly. What a luxury to sleep late. Cool white plastered walls surrounded me, and the bright warm light through the window made a square on the creamy wall. A blue vase on the ledge held one wildflower that I had found in the fields last evening when we arrived. The white petals had just opened and I could smell the warm fragrance around me. The linen curtains blew gently and I closed my eyes again. The sunlight was warm.

I thought about the last three hectic months of my life. Quincy, Illinois, had been my assignment for practice teaching. It was the last step before I graduated and received my degree and teaching credential. The convent at Quincy looked like it had been built by the same architects who built the motherhouse. Large, brick, and square, it surrounded a courtyard that had no name. The building housed the convent and the high school, which was also a girl's boardinghouse.

Quincy was a three-hour drive from St. Louis along the Mississippi River. One of my classmates came with me, S. Judith from the Mankato province. Even though she was from the same province as Maribeth and Joan, she had never heard of them. The convent had only one extra bedroom, so Judith and I roomed together. All those years of learning about teaching and getting my credential was easy compared to actually teaching. I spent a few weeks watching other teachers in my fields of English and music. They were excellent teachers, and I was confident I would be excellent also. That is, until I stood in front of a classroom of senior girls and tried to impart my knowledge to them. I thought I did a good job. It wasn't till years later that I realized I didn't have

184

the slightest interest in whether they were listening or not.

But if teaching meant knowing the subject well and talking about it, then I did an admirable job. I was busy from morning until night. I worked on lesson plans for the classes and tried to get to know the sisters at the convent. They were busy too, and we only said a few words to each other at the end of the day.

I played the guitar at the Saturday evening Mass and accompanied a little choir at the altar, which was a new thing in the liturgy. I wrote music for our Masses at the convent. Sometimes I went to the church down the street and played the organ. I had never been so busy. I remember lying in bed at night, always worried about the next day and how well I would teach. I never wondered if this was the life for me. I had forgotten a long time ago about my father asking if I was happy.

But now the twelve weeks were over. All those soon-to-be-forgotten names of students and the worry about doing a good job was finished. I laid in bed and was just thankful that all the work was done. I had no idea what this day of freedom would bring and I didn't care. I just wanted to watch the patch of sun move down the wall.

I got bored quickly, though, and finally got up. I found Judith reading a book after breakfast and we decided to go for a hike along the bluffs. We hiked down the long lawn to the river trail. It was June but still cool in the morning, so we walked a few miles down the path with wildflowers at our side, and the buzzing of thousands of tiny insects. We saw a black snake slide across the path in front of us. It was probably a water moccasin, a poisonous snake, so we looked carefully before we kept going. We finally got to a clear area of rocks overlooking the river. We walked out on a large flat ledge that jutted out from the bluffs.

I took off my veil and lay down in the sunlight. I could hear the river below and feel the heat of the day when the breeze stopped. Birds cheeped and twittered and the noise blended together with the buzzing of insects and the sounds from the barges on the river and the traffic below on the river road. We crawled over to the edge and looked down. There was nothing below us for hundreds of feet except for the river, a wet brown ribbon below us. I backed away quickly.

We stayed and talked a little longer, but I had heard all the sounds I wanted to hear and it was almost lunchtime. We started back down the path. We walked around a curve and saw three very large black snakes in front of us, sunning themselves on the path. They didn't show any sign of moving. We watched them for a few minutes, then decided to try our luck going around them. My legs got scratched from going through the brush but it was better than getting bitten. We had no sooner gotten on the path again than a huge snake slithered across the path in front of us. And we still had a mile to go. The heat was rising and all the snakes were coming out to sun themselves. We passed two more snakes on large rocks on our left, and we moved as silently as we could, giving them a wide berth. Two more slid into the bushes ahead of us. We kept walking quickly. All I could think of was that I wanted to get back and I wouldn't be going along this path ever again. A lone black snake curled up on the next rock. I couldn't see his head, but his body was big. As big as my hands could fit around. Before we got back to the retreat house we had seen fourteen snakes, and that was more than I ever wanted to see in my lifetime. The rest of the day was blessedly uneventful and all I did was sit around the house and read fun books and waste my time. It was glorious.

The next morning we left for home, and drove down to the two-lane river road. Judith grabbed my arm and said, "Look, that's where we were yesterday."

I looked up to where she was pointing. There was an overhang high above us, about twenty feet of flat rock that had absolutely nothing underneath it and looked like it would break off and come tumbling down on the highway below. I cringed when I saw it. That's where we had laid out in the sun and had crawled over to the edge to see the river below. If I had known that there was nothing underneath us but air, I would have run screaming back to safety on the path, even with all the snakes. I watched where we had been for a long time, looking over my shoulder out the rear window until we turned away from the river and it disappeared from view.

We were headed back to the motherhouse for the summer where we would wait for our assignments to go out on mission. I hoped I wouldn't get a mission with just three sisters, though they

186

were very common. One nun might be elderly, another the principal of the elementary school, and then a young nun who had just come out on mission. That was the usual set-up. My chances were better than most of my classmates to get a larger mission, since I would be a high school teacher. But for now there was no more studying, no more books, and our summer job was to clean the college happily, or at least without complaining, before we left. My two days of total relaxation were gone, and I had no idea when I'd ever have any more.

Chapter 51
Mission

I had graduated at the top of my class of thirty and got the award for best English major. It wasn't as impressive as it sounds because there was only one other English major.

But it was over. I wrote the Mass for our graduation and still have a recording of it. Transferred over the years from large tape to cassette to CD to iTunes. It's a little scratchy but still sounds good to me.

When we returned from practice teaching, the next few weeks were devoted to cleaning the college. There was no cleaning crew--just us, the graduating seniors. I suppose it was a much-needed lesson in humility. We had many of those lessons, but I'm not sure I ever learned the virtue.

No superior ever said this out loud, but I imagine this is what they were thinking. "You graduated. You have a degree and credential. You're a teacher now. But you're not so special that you can't clean!"

We got the message. Every wall had to be cleaned, every floor had to be washed, buffed, and polished. I remember dripping sweat from the summer heat for eight hours a day. Prayers were a welcome relief.

One afternoon in August, I trudged back to our study hall at the far end of the motherhouse with my equally exhausted classmates, and on the bulletin board our teaching assignments for the next year were posted.

I ran my finger down to my name and across. "St. Francis Borgia High School. Washington, Missouri."

The Borgias? Weren't they the evil ones in history? Oh, yeah, there was a saint in there somewhere, I remember. Probably paid for by their incredible wealth. I had never heard of the city of Washington, but it was still somewhere in the state, and had a grade school and a high school. I figured there would be plenty of sisters and I breathed a sigh of relief.

I asked around and discovered the town was on the Missouri River, about an hour away from St. Louis, so I would be able to see my family often. I was excited to tell them. At least I wouldn't be hundreds of miles away.

I had one last home visit before I left for Washington. I stayed in my tiny bedroom for a week. My parents still lived in Jennings, even though the neighborhood had changed dramatically in the four years. A few black families had moved in and the area was experiencing a mass exodus of whites. I wondered how long my parents would stay, but they showed no interest in leaving.

It felt so different at home. Besides the fact that my bedroom had shrunk significantly, I had become a stranger in my childhood home.

My parents couldn't understand why I was still in the convent and I couldn't really explain why I was staying either. If I had told them any one of the repressive things that had happened in the last four years, they would have been shocked and insist that I leave immediately. I knew deep inside of me that they were right, but all those horrible incidents were a thing of the past now, ancient history. I was ready for a new life with forward-looking, liberal people.

There were already a few of my classmates who had left the order and wouldn't be going out on mission with the rest of us. Pam had left in January of our senior year. She told me a few days before Christmas.

"Susie, when I was out at a mission in St. Charles a few weekends ago, that's when I decided to leave."

She looked at me sadly, and in true Pam fashion, she went on with the story.

"You know, it's all white out there in St. Charles, and I was sitting in this circle of old white nuns one Saturday night in the parlor and they were all watching Lawrence Welk on TV, which was awful."

I nodded my head in agreement. I had to watch Lawrence Welk with my grandfather many Friday nights in high school and it was excruciating!

Pam went on. "I had this vision."

I looked up in surprise. A vision? That didn't sound like Pam!

She went on quickly. "It wasn't a vision like that. Nothing supernatural or anything. No Jesus or Mary or anybody like that. I had a vision of me in this group of old white nuns watching Lawrence Welk every Saturday night for the rest of my life. Susie, I lost my vocation right then. That was it. It was over!"

After we both laughed, she went on, "I called my daddy and told him to pick me up fast--the next day. He was coming to pick me up in his station wagon and I could hardly wait to get out of there. I saw this car going past the convent--it was a station wagon—just like his--and I ran outside and down the street after it. I thought he had missed the building! My veil was flying and I was tripping over my shoes, and I wondered what people would think of a black nun running wildly down the street after a car. And it turned out that it wasn't even my daddy. It was some old white guy who really thought I was crazy. I just wanted to be out of there so bad."

I laughed at her story but knew at the same time that she was serious. Being the only black in the middle of an old German community proved an insurmountable barrier. She wanted to be living in and working for her own black community, not the nuns.

After she left we lost track of each other. She wanted to leave the convent life and friends behind. I knew she was teaching in a Catholic school in Illinois somewhere, but we never talked to each other. It would be years before we met again.

My good friend Patrice had left the order right after she graduated and was teaching grade school somewhere in Southern California. I missed her, but she would have been gone on a mission anyway.

Louise was still in, but she was just going into her senior year, and besides, our friendship wasn't the same as it had been when it was forbidden. She had her friends and I had mine.

I was beginning to get a glimpse of what this life would be like. I had dreams of more freedom and more rights for women and nuns in the church, but I began to realize that whatever friends I made, and how wonderful the friendship might be, it would be over as soon as one of us got transferred. There might be more freedom, but there would be no lasting friendships.

I wanted to choose my own roommates, and I wanted my hard-earned friendships to last, but that would never happen.

The day came for me to leave for Washington, MO. The

190

day was already sweltering from the 90 degree heat and humidity. There were only about ten of us left from our class. The others had already left for their assignments.

From where I was sitting in the study hall I saw two nuns came into the office. Sister Rose called my name. Sister Patricia and Sister Janine were here to pick me up for the hour ride to my new home.

My trunk, waiting in the corridor, was loaded in the car by a maintenance man from the high school next door, and I said a last silent goodbye to the motherhouse. I was thrilled to leave and start my real life as a sister in the order.

Chapter 52
Washington, Missouri

We took Highway 44 out of St. Louis, but soon got on Highway 100, a two-lane road that wound through farmland, the deep brown topsoil of Missouri blurring by us. S. Patricia was driving, and S. Janine sat next to her in the front seat. I sat in the back with my books. They asked a few questions, but soon started talking about school-related topics that I knew nothing about. I just watched out the window.

As we drove the long distance, I was glad that my mom had insisted I learn to drive. Maybe I would be able to drive the convent car back and forth from the city.

We stopped at a three-story brick building on Cedar Street, across from the church, with its high steeple shimmering in the heat. The convent was part of larger complex that took up two blocks. Directly across the street was the church. To our right was the high school and across from that the elementary school. The church property took up the entire block.

The two sisters helped pull my heavy trunk out and up the narrow stairs to the second floor.

The convent was old, with dark wood paneling, but neat and clean. I glimpsed a large sitting area with soft fabric chairs and wooden end tables and a non-descript purple and grey carpet underneath.

My bedroom was larger than any room I had ever called my own, especially the tiny cubicle in the dorms for the past four years, even larger than my old bedroom at home. A large window overlooked a field with a few trees at each end. I soon discovered the band would practice there for football season--not my favorite kind of music. A twin bed was under the window, next to it a desk and chair, a few bookshelves, a small cabinet for my clothes, and a white wooden door. A door I could close. I could be alone, really alone, for the first time in four years. It was a great feeling.

The convent was large, with around thirty sisters living there. A cook, a few retired sisters, the superior, Sister Janine, and the rest of us staffed the elementary and high school.

I unpacked a little and hung up all my clothes, all three sets of them. Dark blue skirts, white blouses. I still looked like a nun. Skirt below the knees, regulation plain white blouse, and a small blue veil. But our hair could show in the front, and that was progress. That was a lot of progress, and I was looking forward to so much more.

I put a few of my college textbooks on the shelf, some writing notebooks, my favorite records of Van Cliburn and Glenn Gould, and all my sheet music.

I walked downstairs through the large sitting room to a small parlor. It had an upright piano in it. I lifted the lid. The keys were real ivory, but yellow with age. I played a few notes. Out of tune, but it was all I had. I hoped there was a better piano in the high school, but I might not be able to practice as much on it, due to schedules. I would find out soon.

I found Sister Patricia in the typing room, which was filled with ten typewriters on long tables. She was working.

"Can I walk down to the river? Who do I need to tell?"

"Oh, it's fine as long as someone knows where you are. Like me. I'd come with you, but I need to finish this order."

"Oh, that's fine. I think I can find the river."

"Dinner's at five." She smiled. "Don't get lost."

It was four o'clock already, and the day had started to cool as I walked out the front door, but it was still sticky.

I was glad I had a short skirt and blouse instead of the suffocating habit.

A large brick building loomed over the entire next block. Its windows were so dirty and thick with cobwebs that I couldn't see inside. An old faded sign, "Meerschaum Corn Cob Pipes" stretched along the whole side of the building.

Before I came to Washington, I learned that the town was the corn-cob pipe capitol of the world. Quite a distinction, I suppose. I kept walking down past the closed train station, crossed the railroad tracks, and came to the banks of the Missouri river.

It was beautiful, in its own brown and wild way. The Mississippi was a slow-moving giant. This river was wild and unruly with currents making giant swirls, quickly replaced with others. It pulsated with power, the water churning in one direction and then another as it pushed past. The banks were covered with trees, overgrown and hanging into the water. I loved it. Living by a river again was my dream. And maybe this river, freer and wilder, would be a sign of my new life in this new mission. I hoped so. I promised myself I would walk down a few times every week.

I got back to the convent in time for dinner and was introduced to everyone. It would take a while to remember everyone. The only people I remember from that night were the sisters who drove me from the motherhouse, and Sister Juan, a young, tall, dark-haired nun who taught art and whose bedroom was next to mine upstairs.

I saw the high school the next day, walking through the gloomy tiled hallways that smelled of cleaning solution. St. Francis Borgia was a co-ed Catholic high school. Its only rival in town was the public high school, and they competed in football, band, and scholastic awards. Our school was very proud of its reputation. In a town of only ten thousand that was important.

I couldn't, or didn't want to, imagine the school filled with students. There would be so many. And for all my classes and degree and credential, I had no idea what to do when I stood in front of a classroom full of teenagers.

I used my new key to open the band room. Sister Clare was the orchestra and band teacher, and I would be teaching the chorus. The thought of it made my stomach do flip-flops. I had no idea what to do. I was a pianist, not a vocalist.

The band room was big and had a stale smell of sweat. A desk was up against the back wall. I walked over to it and sat down. This would be my desk that I would share with Sister Clare. Fear gripped me as I imagined all the students who would be thinking I knew how to teach.

The next day I walked across the street to the church. It had a lingering odor of incense. My new key opened a little door to wooden steps leading up to the choir loft. On the landing was a beautiful stained- glass window. I had loved stained glass for as long as I can remember, but because the window was on the enclosed staircase and landing--the only person who could ever see the beautiful glass was the one walking up the stairs.

I had two weeks to prepare my lesson plans for the first week. I worked hard every night, reading all the stories from the

194

literature textbooks and imagining thoughtful and vibrant discussions. I typed study sheets and mimeographed material. I had English, music appreciation and religion classes. I wanted to make religion an interesting subject, not the stilted rules of centuries past, but real questions about what we believed. I was over-prepared and excited. I felt confident that the students would learn so much from me. The first day was a blur. Hundreds of students, names, roll calls, making sure everyone was in the correct class, names spelled and pronounced correctly. Books handed out, nothing to teach yet.

When I think back to my standing there, in front of each class, I'm sure they could see right through my fake confidence and bravado and know that this was my first teaching assignment. But most of the students were polite and sweet. It was the late sixties, and the rebellions of Woodstock and the college campuses and the demonstrations hadn't quite reached the farming communities of the Midwest. If anything, they were bored, not rebellious.

But I did okay. In fact, I was proud of how well I taught. The students would learn so much from me. I was teaching really well. The discussions weren't going as well as I had hoped, but I was giving them lots of my knowledge.

About a month later I gave my first test to the students. They did horribly. Every one of them. Even the sweet girls in the front seats who listened carefully.

I had somehow forgotten that there were living, breathing students in front of me, and that I had to reach them. It wasn't all about me, and how well I presented or knew the material.

After the first test, I became the student. A student of teaching. And I began to realize I wasn't a very good one. But I did want to learn.

I would often walk down to the river. It was beautiful at any time of the year. Not that I had too much time to spend watching the river. I taught religion, World Literature, creative writing and chorus, plus numerous piano lessons. We put on two plays when I was there, "My Fair Lady" and "Fiddler on the Roof. Both were excellent musicals for high school, if you had a cast good enough to do them, and we were lucky to have that. Our musicals weren't good because of me. The tradition of band, chorus, and drama had been built up over the years and I simply had to maintain that tradition.

I loved having my own room in the convent. It was such a contrast to the dorms I had lived in that I was overjoyed. And I was by myself--not having to listen to all the sounds of thirty or more people in the same dorm. The thrill of having my own space, of being able to close the door after a difficult teaching day, was heaven to me. I bought a multi-colored shag rug, my first purchase in four years, and decorated my room with flowers in a few vases.

There were so many sisters at the convent that I had my choice of friends. Sister Clare was the band teacher and Sister Inez was the drama director. I had new friends and wasn't particularly interested in keeping track of my old friends. It was hard to teach and to keep up with all those different people in so many places. There just wasn't time to practice the art of friendship. And I was learning that no matter how many friends I may have thought I had, they would all leave in the end. Building a community didn't mean much when I would be broken up a year or two later and you'd have to start over again. The reality of community was completely different than the loving picture that had been drawn for us.

I made one non-convent friend too. I met Jenny at a parent-teacher meeting. She was the mother of ten children, and she was so friendly and nice that I started going over to her house often after school. I think she liked the adult conversation! The first fall I was there we made apple butter in her basement, a big vat of it that had to be tended for hours. Jenny ran her family like a little army. Fifteen minutes in the bathroom at night per child starting at 7:00 pm for the youngest. She was a wonderful person who thrived on being a mother. It was a role I wasn't interested in, but she was great at it. The year was off to a good start.

Chapter 53
The Christmas Concert

The first few months in Washington, Mo. went by in a blur. My life seemed to consist of waking up, prayers, Mass, a quick breakfast, hurrying to school, endless classes in the same classroom, going home, eating dinner, preparing for the next day, and, blessedly, going to sleep. I would sometimes glance out my window to the trees in the park next door, but I didn't even have much time to do that.

S. Clare asked me one afternoon in November if I would like to play in the community Christmas concert. The mayor played the string bass in the orchestra, but they needed one more bass player.

I always had loved the string bass. I had played it once during our "Introduction to the Orchestra" class in the convent. It was a requirement for a music degree. I almost felt part of the instrument, even more than playing the piano. I loved holding it close and drawing the bow back and forth. There was only one problem. I couldn't play it.

I suppose in one sense I could. I could pull the bow over the open strings, E, A, D, and G and make a beautiful rich sound, but I couldn't play any of the notes in between.

Laughing, I told S. Clare my dilemma, the reason I could never play in the orchestra, and she said, "That's ok. You'll do fine. And I've already signed you up. I hope you don't mind."

If I had been prone to panic attacks, I would have had one, but I couldn't even use that as an excuse. There I was, signed up to be in an orchestra for the first time in my life, only I couldn't play the instrument. How I had wanted to be the piano soloist with an orchestra, playing some famous piano concerto by Beethoven or Rachmaninoff, but not this.

Oh well, I could read notes and I was a good musician. I had a great sense of timing and I hoped that would be enough. After all, how many notes could there be in Christmas Carols?

The Washington Community Orchestra consisted of about 25-30 volunteers. I had never heard them play, and I had no idea what to expect.

Clare dragged me to the first rehearsal in November. She was playing the violin. But she knew how to play it! I smiled at everyone as I painstakingly lifted up and tuned the large instrument. I had at least learned how to do that.

The mayor said hello and took his place next to me. My face was already as red as some of the Christmas decorations, in anticipation of my imminent embarrassment, and I figured it would turn green before long, to add to the seasonal colors. I prayed that the mayor, of all people, wouldn't notice how terrible I was.

The first piece, "Hark the Herald Angels Sing" started on G, an open string, went to D, another open string, and had a few A's scattered throughout, and I didn't have to put my finger down on a string to be completely embarrassed at being out-of-tune.

I prayed that the rest of the carols would be so simple. A few pieces later, there was a song that started in the Key of C. Now that was impossible. I made the quick decision to sit it out and let the mayor carry it. To join in meant that I would have had to PLAY the instrument.

The few weekly rehearsals went by quickly. My confidence grew rapidly, not because I learned how to play. It grew because I knew when to play and when to shut up. And no one ever seemed to notice.

The mayor was off to my side, and I don't think he ever glanced over or guessed that I was missing more than fifty percent of the notes- more like seventy-five to be honest.

We had a very successful Christmas concert, and although I wasn't proud of my part, at least I hadn't been completely humiliated. It was quite a success, in those terms. I still love the richness and depth of the string bass. I'm just very glad I've never had the opportunity to "play" it again.

Chapter 54
Teaching

A few years ago, Malcolm Gladwell came up with an interesting concept: that it takes ten thousand hours of practice to become an expert--at anything.

I understand that from playing the piano. The first year is difficult, and most people give up after a few months. Learning the notes, trying to remember them and where they are, timing, putting both hands together and making them work independently. It takes forever to play a recognizable tune. Luckily most of my students, including myself, were young when we started, and gradually built the skill just by putting in the time. I had no expectations when I was five, and by the time I got to that "critical" age, when I did have expectations, I already knew how to play.

I think a person needs ten thousand hours of practice to become a good teacher. During those first few months in Washington I was beginning to realize that perhaps I wasn't quite the excellent teacher I had hoped to be. I don't recall making any drastic changes though. I just kept teaching and trying hard to make the classes interesting. But in reality, I was in an ocean, just keeping my head above water, barely breathing. I couldn't swim. I didn't even know where the shore was.

I had two successes that first year. The first one was that I showed up every day and tried.

And the second success had nothing to do with teaching. Two students, football players in my senior English class, were yelling at each other as I walked in the door one morning.

"Miller."

"No, Bud!" over and over. The fight had almost gotten to the punching stage. I put my books down hard on the desk, walked up to them, both 6'4" at least, grabbed their collars, and pulled them apart.

"Not in my English class! If you want to fight about whether Miller or Budweiser is the best, you can wait and do it AFTER class. Now sit down!"

And I pushed them into their chairs and started class. No one said a word.

I never found out whether Miller or Bud was the best, since I didn't drink beer. But showing up for classes and breaking up a fight were my two successes that first year.

Chapter 55
Fiddler on the Roof

It was a few days before our spring musical, the "Fiddler on the Roof." The senior musical was the big event of the year, not only in the high school, but in the town of Washington. Over three hundred students tried out for the leads, the chorus, or the band. We never had to ask for volunteers because it was the social event of the town. The Catholic school prided itself on putting on the best musical, far superior to anything the public high school had to offer, and I had to follow in that tradition. Luckily, there were so many students trying out that we found some good leads. Wayne was only a junior, but he was perfect for Tevye. He had that sense of humor, that "attitude," and all we had to do was put on a few fake pounds and a beard and he was pretty close. No Zero Mostel, but it was only a high school production, after all.

On Wednesday afternoon before the weekend of the play, Sister Linda, our principal, called me into the office. When I got there, Sister Inez and Sister Clare were already sitting there quietly. Sister Linda started to speak. "Wayne was caught last night at school defacing the property and has been suspended indefinitely. I wanted to let the three of you know about this first because he can't be in the play."

"What did he do," I asked in desperation, thinking maybe we could come up with something to salvage the play. I was shocked; not shocked that Wayne would do something wrong, but that he would do it a few days before the play.

"He and a few other boys were drinking, got cans of green and white paint, dipped boots in them, put them on long poles and made footprints on the ceilings of the high school. They've spent the whole morning cleaning the corridors."

I nodded mutely. I remember almost smiling. It must have been pretty hilarious to see those footprints on the ceiling. I couldn't very well plead for a drunken stupid junior to be let back in school. There was obviously no doubt as to his guilt and policy was policy.

But what about the play? We had sold thousands of tickets and now we were minus the lead. And if you've ever seen "Fiddler on the Roof", which I hope you have because it's a wonderful musical, you know that Tevye is not just the main character, he's also the soul of the play.

Luckily we had an understudy who had rehearsed the lines so often with Wayne that he filled in quite well, although it was a shaky production. I held my breath opening night, worried about what else could possibly go wrong. The chorus did well under my direction, and the band supported them and we somehow got through the two weekends of the play. I don't remember if I was numb at that point, but I thought it had gone as well as it possibly could have.

Chapter 56
Freedom Summer

I went to California to visit my friend Patrice the summer of 1971, after my first year of teaching in Washington. I wasn't teaching summer school and asked for two weeks off to go to San Francisco. I don't really know why Sister Janine gave me permission, but sisters were leaving at an alarming rate, and maybe she didn't want me hanging around doing nothing all summer except being resentful. Maybe that's why I got to go. Or maybe she just didn't care anymore.

Patrice met me at the San Francisco airport. She had been a year ahead of me, had left the order and was teaching grade school in California.

By the time we drove an hour to her parent's house in Pleasanton, I knew I wouldn't be dressed like a nun for very long. Her parents were on vacation for two weeks, and we stayed at their house outside San Francisco. I bought two pairs of white bell-bottom jeans that afternoon, a few colorful tops, and changed into them as quickly as I could. The veil got packed in my suitcase.

I was free. I looked like an ordinary person. For someone like me, who always prided myself on being different, smarter, more elite, I was thrilled to finally be "ordinary."

We went to a big mall and walked for hours, window shopping. Nobody knew I was a nun. Nobody stared at me like I was strange or out-of-place. No one even noticed me. It was glorious.

We went to movies and Fisherman's Wharf. We explored San Francisco, a beautiful city. We ran on the sand and in the waves. I knew I'd be going back to teach in a few weeks, but it was nice to be free--even for a short time.

For all my new-found freedom, I didn't really think about leaving the order. I had just become a teacher, and I had made a commitment. Life was certainly better out on mission. I had friends--the community of thirty sisters was a great size. I could ignore the ones I didn't like and make friends with the ones I did like. I didn't have to worry about particular friendships anymore.

Patrice and I had an amazing two weeks. She had to go

back to San Gabriel, in Southern California, where she taught in the grade school. That's why we were able to drive down Pacific Coast Highway. I'd been few places in my life, and none so beautiful as that drive down the coast. I was a little afraid of the highway, coupled with Patrice's driving which seemed too fast, but when I dared to look, the views were spectacular. We pulled off at every viewpoint we could to stare at the ocean, which was an endless source of wonder for me--its changing moods and colors. But I had to leave all too soon and get back to reality. I saw my parents for a week, then headed back to Washington for my second year of teaching.

When my dad asked his usual question, I replied honestly that I was happy. I was content. Life was incredibly busy, but I was teaching and trying to get better at it. I settled in for a long year.

Chapter 57
Decision

In September, a few of us went into St. Louis for the afternoon, and went to a Saturday evening Mass at a parish church I had never attended before. It was a typical seventies attempt at modern architecture, the tall soaring building, tall windows with a few modern stained-glass windows. The altar had its requisite statues of saints, and chrysanthemums lined the altar, probably from a funeral that week.

The Mass was boring as usual. I half-listened to a sermon. I don't remember it at all, but I do remember right after the sermon, a thought came to me.

I wouldn't be here next year. I was going to leave. I knew it was right. It was true. It wasn't even a real decision. It was just a fact that suddenly was stuck in my head. I was going to leave at the end of this year. Just like that. Decision made. After all the scolding and screaming and tears and friendships and worry and prayer and hopes for the future, it didn't seem like it any of those things that brought me to a decision. I had simply decided to leave.

I remember the drive back to Washington that evening. The green trees were a blur by the side of the road as the other sisters in the car talked. I was strangely quiet. All I could think about was the "decision" I had made. And I had made it. There was no second-guessing, no weighing of options, no going back. It was done.

When we got home, I walked into my room and looked at my multi-colored rug that I had bought a year ago. That would come with me. My notebooks of writings I would take, but most of the books could stay.

What would I do? I had no idea, but I was sure I could get a teaching job somewhere. Maybe they'd want me to stay here? No, probably not. But there would be jobs available almost anywhere. I had my Missouri teaching credential for high school English, music and religion. My parents would be thrilled. I wouldn't tell them yet.

I couldn't believe that I could throw away six years of this life so quickly, without a thought. But that's what had happened. I never second-guessed my decision, not in any of the weeks to come.

I knocked on S. Janice's office door early in October.

"I want to let you know I'll be leaving this June. I'd like to ask for a leave of absence."

That's what everybody asked for. A leave of absence to think things over. No one ever came back.

She looked up at me with a blank expression on her face.

"Well, you have to write to the archbishop to revoke your vows. I'll give you the address."

She never said anything about my staying. Was I that bad of a person? Was I that horrible of a teacher? All my fears and anxieties and inadequacies came rushing to me at once. Was she not going to put up at least some resistance? If she had said, "Oh, I'm sorry, we really hate to see you go. Please reconsider," it would have meant so much to me. But she said nothing. I remember walking out of her office, not feeling bad about leaving, but that she didn't care whether I left or not.

Chapter 58
Why I left

I never questioned my decision to leave in the months afterwards. But the idea didn't come out of nowhere. It came from years of ridicule, of humiliation, of conforming instead of rebelling, of being made to think I wasn't important or worthwhile as myself.

The Catholic church made a mistake when it elected Pope John the twenty-third. They thought he would be an interim pope, a place holder who would do nothing. They had never been so wrong.

He called the Second Vatican Council, the first council since 1869. It took the ancient, conservative church and pushed it into the modern world.

I was thrilled with the direction the church was taking, and I naively thought it would continue.

At the same time, during my senior year in high school, I got to know Sister Rachel, an independent, free-spirited, intelligent sister who did pretty much what she wanted and lived her own life, even in the convent. I thought she was the model for what sisters would be in the future. During that window of time right after the council, it looked like she represented the future.

No one knew the battles that lay ahead. The sisters working in the fields of education and medicine knew a lot more than I did. We as students in the motherhouse knew almost nothing about the war that was being fought behind the scenes in the church.

The sisters who ran the order knew that no women at all had been allowed in the council sessions in Rome. No woman had a voice or a vote on anything related to the future of the church, and the few sisters that were finally allowed to attend a few years later were observers only, not even allowed to speak.

I entered with false hopes, buoyed up by the words of the council, that we were all called to holiness, to be equal before God, that marriage was just as holy as being a priest or nun. I believed the future was bright.

After six years and a new pope, the church reforms ground quickly to a halt. They were stopped by the conservative majorities of the hierarchy. Many sisters strove to have a voice in the church, but they were silenced.

For us teachers in the convent, it was a battle that we were only dimly aware of. Our instructions were the same. We were taught by the same repressive standards of the past, all the while giving lip service to the message of the council. Things were changing. We had new habits. We talked about new ideas all the time.

There were shining lights, women who were powerful, intelligent, well-spoken leaders, but their voices were difficult to hear. They were barely loud enough to hear in the motherhouse.

The order was an odd mix of women. We were all college-educated, leaders in our fields of education, entrusted with running large educational and medical organizations, yet not good enough to be leaders of our own communities--or our own lives. We were all still under the will of the priests and bishops, the all-male hierarchy of the church.

I became aware of this slowly, like a dark shadow lengthening.

I wanted to be free. I had no dreams anymore of reforming the church. Not once in my six years of training had I been of any use to anyone. I wanted to help people. And I wanted was to choose my own roommates. I didn't want money or marriage; I wanted nothing more than the choice to make decisions about my life.

The Catholic Church believed the massive exodus of nuns was the horrible influence of a secular world, the temptation of sex and permissiveness which had become the norm--the Woodstock, free-love generation.

But the exodus had many causes. Some of it was feminism and women wanting to be equal to men, but more of it was the way the church treated the sisters. We were definitely second-class citizens and had never been anything else.

It's 2021 as I write this, and Pope Francis announced recently that "women will never become priests." We as women have come a long way in parts of the world, but not in the church. I'm glad I got out when I did.

I had two choices. I could stay and fight for the right to be heard, to make my own decisions. I knew it would be a lifelong war, just to win a few small battles. Or I could simply walk out the door and be free. No one to tell me what to do, what to think, how to dress, how to live, what to say, where to go, what was right or wrong.

In the end, there was no choice.

I think that's why my decision was so easy that day, and why it came so quickly. The only question was why it had taken so long.

Chapter 59
The Moody Blues

All my life I've been a musical snob. My favorite composers are Bach, Chopin, Mozart and Beethoven. I loved playing their pieces on the piano and looked down on people who didn't appreciate classical music. I never bothered listening to the Beatles, and I hated Elvis, although he did have a nice voice.

But there was one group I loved when I was in the convent-
-The Moody Blues. They had recorded music with the London Symphony Orchestra, and I thought they were trying to join classical and rock. In retrospect, I think they just used the London Symphony as a background, but at the time I was excited at the possibilities.

I would go down to the basement and listen to their records while working on my lesson plans. We only had one record player in the whole convent! I would listen all evening.

When I read in our intact newspaper that they were coming to St. Louis, I dreamt that I might be able to go, but I wasn't sure how I could manage it.

I had requested, as a junior sister, to see Van Cliburn in concert, but we were never allowed to go anywhere, not a classical concert, or even a religious concert. I was quite sure that S. Janine would never let me go to a "rock" concert. However, I had already told her I was leaving, so I guess I couldn't be any more corrupted than I already was.

And I guess I sold it pretty well--I'm sure I mentioned the London Symphony.

She said yes. I could go, but I had to find someone to go with me, so I asked Sister Juan, my artist friend. She didn't care about the music. She was just glad to get out.

We were going to see the Moody Blues on a Saturday night at the Arena in St. Louis. The arena was a huge indoor stadium where hockey teams played. We would be very late driving back, so we would stay in a convent close by in the city and drive back in the morning.

I sent in the money and the tickets arrived a few weeks later in the mail. We were really going!

I had been to many concerts in high school. My dad had taken me on the bus downtown to see Van Cliburn--I even got his autograph. And I saw Philippe Entremont, a great French pianist. Piano players were like movie stars to me. They had to be excellent pianists--and good-looking!

My friend Martha and I had bought tickets to see Rudolf Nureyev and Margot Fonteyn when we were juniors in high school. I remember standing at the pay phone in the noisy cafeteria at school. We called the ticket office over and over again the day the tickets went on sale till we got through. We only had our lunch hour to call! And we got the tickets. They were expensive and I don't remember how we managed it, but we were high up in the balcony. Martha and I didn't care. We were going to see Nureyev! I persuaded my mom to drive us downtown that Saturday evening and Martha and I wore our best skirts and blouses--no match for the fashionably elite of St. Louis, but we didn't care that we looked like poor high school students. That's what we were.

Nureyev and Fonteyn danced to Khachaturian's "Gayaneh" which will always be one of my favorite ballets and just to see Nureyev dance in person was an unforgettable experience. No one has ever matched his brilliance and magnificence on stage.

But it had been six long years since I had been to any concert.

Sister Juan and I drove into the city, found a parking place at the huge arena, and joined thousands of young people pushing into the entrance. We were dressed in our new "modern" habits, blue skirt, white blouse, and black veil. We weren't quite as modern as our fellow concert goers, who were dressed in psychedelic jeans, flowing peasant blouses and flowers in their long hair. We climbed up and up and finally found our seats. The young couple next to us looked at us strangely but didn't say anything. And then the music started.

The arena had a large metal roof high above us, and smoke filled the whole building. It wasn't cigarette smoke. It had a strange, fruity smell, and was very distinctive.

The concert was loud, but mellow as far as rock music. The Moody Blues were known for their melodies and gentle harmonies rather than the wildness of other bands. It was still exciting and amazing to me. I remember toward the end someone on stage passed out and the music stopped while they got a stretcher and took the person out. He seemed to be part of the ensemble, but not a lead singer. Then they played their last sets to tremendous applause.

As we were trying to get out with the crowds after the program, Juan and I got separated.

"I'll meet you at the car," I yelled.

She heard me and shouted "Okay."

The couple next to me, smiling and wearing flowers, said, "Hey, cool costume."

And then they laughed. "Hey, wow, you look like a real nun!"

I just smiled. It had been dark and smoke-filled inside, but now I was in the floodlights that lit up the parking lot, in full view. I didn't think I had breathed too much of the smoky air inside the arena, but I felt paranoid, like everyone was staring at me. I decided that it was because everyone was staring at me. Yes, I was a nun. And yes, I felt completely out of place. And yes, I had already decided to leave. I only had eight more months of this. I had felt out of place many times in the last six years; at the doctor's office, on the bus once, whenever I went home for a visit, at the mall where I would go with my mom, but I had never felt this different from everyone.

I learned that nuns don't usually go to Moody Blues concerts, and they don't inhale three hours-worth of marijuana smoke.

That night I fell asleep easily, my habit thrown on the chair next to the bed in the little guest room, and dreamt of freedom.

Chapter 60
Creative Writing Class

During January of my second year of teaching, I had an opportunity to teach a creative writing class to seniors. I jumped at the chance. I loved creative writing, and I knew I could do a good job.

I imagined a class of motivated, intelligent students who really wanted to learn how to write. When I walked into the first class, the room was full. A few sweet eager girls with notebooks and pens, and about fifteen senior boys who had flunked English the year before. They weren't going to college. They didn't need a college prep class. Creative writing sounded easy. And they all signed up.

I looked over my class. I wasn't too disappointed. I really wanted to make a success of it.

Wayne slouched in the front seat, his long blonde hair covering most of his face. We knew each other, since he had been the lead in the school play the previous year--until he got suspended. Gordon and Keith were making spitballs, rolling them between their fingers. Henry stared out the window at the snow piled up on the parking lot.

I told them the requirements for the class. Hand in five writing assignments every week. Five pages each. If you did that, you would get an A.

"Can I get an A, sister?" Wayne's hand shot up. Gordon, Keith and Greg were laughing already.

"Yes, you can, Wayne," and the whole class dissolved into laughter. They all knew Wayne. Many of the boys were just like him.

The other English teachers were a little annoyed with me at our first department meeting.

"You shouldn't be telling those students they can get A's, especially since creative writing isn't even a core class," Sister Frances stated firmly. "Most of them flunked English last year."

I stood up for myself--one of the first times.

"If they do the assignments, then I'm going to give them A's. Why shouldn't they be able to do well in an English class?"

I won that small battle, but I still had to teach the class. The first Friday, 23 notebooks were turned in, and I read through them over the weekend.

I had told them, "If you can't think of anything to write, just write "I don't know what to write" until you think of something. The important thing is to keep writing."

Wayne got that part of the assignment perfectly. The first week all five pages were, "I don't know what to write," but by the second week he described a fly that had landed on his desk. Every detail, including those fascinating eyes. It was actually quite good. I was impressed and gave him an A for the assignment. Wayne didn't get an A for the class, but he did manage to get a well-deserved B, which might have been the best grade he ever received in his short career as a student. He and many others surpassed my expectations and really wrote from their hearts.

Henry Barnes wasn't very smart, but seemed like a nice, quiet kid. He lived with his father on their farm about twenty miles outside of town. One Friday he handed in his notebook. As I read it, I realized that this was what writing was about.

His dad woke him up at 2am one morning. Their cow was giving birth, and they went out to the barn to help in any way they could, since it was still cold.

He described the birth simply, the new life, the warmth, the mother licking the baby, the calf latching onto its mother, the freezing cold of the night, but witnessing the miracle of life. It was simple, beautiful, and honest.

It was a window into the innocence and fascination with new life that Henry, with his Miller beers, football and girls, would never have wanted to admit.

That moment was one of the few times in my short teaching career that I felt I had really connected to a student, or more correctly, helped a student connect to their real self.

Chapter 61
Virtues but Mostly Vices

Sister Patricia was the high school librarian. She was in her thirties, shy with a thin little smile that appeared every so often when the study hall was perfectly silent. But I knew her pretty well, and she wasn't all that shy, and I knew she loved to smoke. Because it was against the rules, she didn't dare smoke in public or even in private, so it limited her to a few carefully chosen moments each year when she was on home visit or when everyone was on vacation, which hardly ever happened.

I had a lot of virtues, humility being the best one, and kindness, and generosity. I could go on, but after I decided to leave the convent, I realized I needed a few vices, so I found Pat one morning in the back of the library.

"Hi, Pat. I have a favor to ask."

"Sure. What is it? Help me get these boxes in here first, though."

"Ok. Well, you know I'm leaving in June, and, I know it sounds dumb, but I thought maybe I should know how to smoke, or at least handle a cigarette properly, you know."

She tried not to laugh. Just then a student walked in with some books and the smile disappeared.

"Sister Susan," she turned away and began to help the student," you can just bring the material to me this evening. I'll be more than glad to help you."

I grinned as I walked to my English class. But the next problem was how to get the cigarettes. Washington was a small town. Everybody knew me, and word would get around pretty quick if I bought a carton of cigarettes at Droeges supermarket. Not to mention that there were probably ten Droege children scattered between the elementary school and high school. I even taught a few.

I got through English class without a glimmer of an idea and headed to the office. I sat down at the long table outside the principal's office, going through some assignments I wanted to duplicate on the office machines.

I could hear the principal really giving it to some poor

unfortunate in the office.

"If this happens one more time... a disgrace to this school... your father..."

Was it Wayne, or Joe? No, probably Gordon. The secretary walked in and put a six pack of Miller beer and two cartons of cigarettes on the table next to me, one of them open.

"Can you believe this!" She sounded deeply offended. "It's that Joe again," she muttered as she went back in her office.

"That's terrible," I stared at the loot.

"He's in so much trouble," I could hear her office chair creaking as she sat down on it.

My eyes focused on the carton of cigarettes. That's it. If only I could get one pack. I can't do that! How ridiculous to even think about it.

Why not? It was as if God had put them there for me. This was my chance. I picked up my books. I didn't have much time because this room was like a freeway interchange between classes. Students and teachers came in at any time with messages, Xerox work, off-campus permits. I got my books in my arms and walked past the table. My hands reached out, fumbled with the carton, got one pack out and slipped it under the top book.

Sister Inez breezed in the door.

"Hi, how's it going?"

"Fine," I whispered. "Just fine," I managed again in a normal voice. I strolled out the door.

I stood next to Pat in the dinner line.

"Got it,"

"What?" She turned to me and then remembered. "Ok. How's ten o'clock. Your room?"

"Fine." I put some mashed potatoes on my plate and didn't say another word. I worked diligently that evening in my room, made all my lesson plans for the next week, corrected papers. At ten I heard a knock on my door. Pat came in quickly. She had matches and a pine air freshener. I locked the door and opened the windows wide.

"Well, here they are. I hope they're the right brand."

"Are you kidding?" She grabbed one cigarette, lit it, and inhaled deeply. "Anything's the right brand when I can get it. Ok,

216

let's get down to business. I'll light it. Now just inhale."

I started coughing. "That's awful. Do they all taste this bad?"

"Well, pretty much so. But you'll get used to it soon enough. Don't worry. No, you're holding it like a pencil. Here, like this."

I smoked one half of a cigarette, muttering a few non-convent approved words, and gave up in a fit of coughing. I couldn't stop. And Pat couldn't stop laughing.

"I'll do you a favor," she finally managed to whisper.

"What?"

"I don't really think that you should learn how to smoke. It's a dirty, nasty, terrible habit. I'll take those cigarettes off your hands. What if someone found out you'd been smoking?"

"It's a deal." I spoke softly so I wouldn't start coughing again.

We aired out the room until it was about the same temperature as the snow outside and it smelled pretty much like pines or springtime and we talked till midnight. Pat got the cigarettes and I started looking for other vices.

Chapter 62
Waiting

After six years of being in the habit, I yearned to be an ordinary person. Which was unusual, because I had always wanted to be an extraordinary person, but not because of some uniform I was wearing. I would have welcomed applause and fame because of my musical ability or some poem I had written, but not just because I was dressed like a nun.

It was good to make friends with other sisters in the convent, but with anyone else on the "outside," it was a problem. People would look at me like I was some kind of freak. If I had the chance to talk to them they might get to know me as a person, but it was difficult. There was always that barrier to get through.

"Gosh, you have a wonderful sense of humor even though you're a nun," or

"Gee, you're very liberal. I didn't expect that!" Every personality trait was unexpected because I was a nun!

I was tired of all the pre-judgments that people made based on their old, tired experience of elementary school nuns with their ever-present rulers. I just wanted to walk down the mall or a street and not have anyone stare at me, like I did in San Francisco that previous summer.

I'd left my home and my parents and lived for six years following someone else's rules and someone else's decisions about my life. I had never been on my own. I never had a job or paid for food and rent. It was great not having to worry about money, but I couldn't make any decisions either. I could never save up for that Nikon camera, or go on a trip, or buy something special for dessert at the store, something that just I wanted.

Going back to my parent's house was not what I wanted, either. I had seen the ones who had left. I had seen them go home, but not too far away from the convent, and they had kept their old convent friends. They were the fish trying to leap out of the fishbowl and never quite making it. Perhaps not the best analogy….

I was ready, finally, to try life on my own. I wrote to my friend Patrice in Los Angeles. She said I could room with her the following year. She was teaching at a San Gabriel elementary school, and there was a high school connected with it. She would write a recommendation for me.

I applied for a job at San Gabriel Catholic High School in San Gabriel, California. They needed an English, music, and religion teacher. It was a perfect fit. I accepted a teaching job for $5,200 a year. I could live on that. I had never earned any real money before, so it seemed like a lot at the time.

I was ready to go. I had a job, and a place to live. I regretted leaving my parents and family, but I knew it would be for just a short time, maybe a year or two. By then, I would be able to support myself and not be dependent on my friends from the convent for my social life.

Chapter 63
If You Don't Succeed at First, Please Don't Try Again

One afternoon about a week before Christmas, I took my coin bag out of my purse and counted my meager supply of money. A few dollars and some change. Just enough, I hoped. I walked out the front door into the icy morning, past the corn cob pipe factory, all the way down to the Missouri River. I loved watching the river in its many moods. It was angry this morning, with ice floes in the whirling grey water. There had been a storm, and lots of debris, tree trunks and branches, were swirling in the water. I took a few pictures with my old camera and walked to Droege's drug store downtown. Actually, Droege's was the downtown, along with a small bank, an auto repair shop, and a tailor.

The store was warm and empty. I picked up some toothpaste and a carton of cigarettes. Mr. Droege's elderly father was at the cash register. I said, "Good morning," and he rang up my purchases. I was looking at the Christmas display on the counter, so I didn't notice if he had a reaction to my unusual purchase. I had only a few more months of my career as a nun, so I didn't really care anymore. They would never kick me out in the middle of a teaching year, and they could yell at me all they wanted. It wouldn't make any difference. And Patricia would be so happy, it was worth it.

He didn't say anything, but put my purchases in the usual paper bag, gave me my change, and I walked home.

Christmas morning, we all gathered after Mass in the large living room, with its Christmas tree, and lots of chairs pulled around so all thirty of us could open our presents together. As we walked in, I nudged Pat.

"You probably shouldn't open that red present here. Take it up to your room."

She was talking to S. Cristeta, and I wasn't sure she heard me.

One of us picked up the presents under the tree and handed them to the right person. It's funny how I don't remember a single present that I got, but I certainly remember Pat's present.

220

She tore off a little of the wrapping on one end, got a little red herself, and tried to cover it up. She set it down on the rug by her chair and picked up another present quickly. No one noticed because we were all opening our own presents.

She looked at me. Thrilled, angry? I couldn't quite tell.

That evening after a lovely Christmas dinner, Pat came to my room.

"Thank you so much! I can't believe you let me open it in front of everyone." She added a few new words to my vocabulary after that. She was a librarian. I don't remember the exact words anymore, but they couldn't have been very bad. We were nuns.

"I tried to warn you, but I guess you weren't listening." The perfect ploy. Blame it on her.

"Okay, you have to learn how to smoke. One more try. I have a whole carton now!"

"I don't want to learn. Really! They're all yours."

"No, you have to try just one more time. Just try one more."

She opened the carton, and the windows in my room. The temperature was in the low thirties. The sky was dark, but the grey clouds threatened snow. We sat on the floor, shivering, and I lit my second cigarette. Yuk! It was by far the second most horrible thing I had ever tasted.

"Breathe it in. You'll get used to it."

"You said that last time, and no, I won't," as I choked and coughed. And cried. It was that bad.

I managed to breathe in a few puffs, and that was it. I was finished.

I think Pat felt terrible, not because I was choking and in distress, but because I had wasted a perfectly good cigarette-- again! She breathed in deeply and savored the moment. Then we tried to wave the extra smoke over to the window, so it wouldn't seep under the door and down the corridor. I finally got to shut my window, Pat went back to her room, and I lay awake for a long time trying to get warm.

So that was my smoking career. I've tried a few things only once or twice in my life. I had wasabi once, mistaking it for green goddess dressing next to my salad at a Japanese restaurant. I never made that mistake again. I've had half a beer, one skiing lesson where I almost died--making it from the bench where I put my skis on to the "Lessons" sign, (a few feet away), and one-half of a cigarette.

Pat, however, enjoyed her Christmas present more than anyone knew--except me. I noticed almost every time I went past her room how it smelled, well, kind of like pine trees in the rain.

Chapter 64
Zithers and Nuns

When we were still in the motherhouse, Pam and I used to make fun of ridiculous obscure rules. We heard about them in our instruction periods because they were still in the rulebooks.

I remember two of them clearly. I'm sure there were many more that I've forgotten.

One was that a School Sister of Notre Dame couldn't get in a boat. Not a big ocean liner, I assume, because none of them would have come to America in the 1800's without the help of boats. I think the rule was about smaller boats, like rowboats. I imagine some nun had drowned after getting in a boat--or falling out of it--so no one was allowed to get in a boat.

Made sense with our old serge habits. Falling into a body of water and trying to get all those clothes off? Impossible. I would have drowned, without a doubt. And maybe there was the modesty issue. I'm sure some nuns would have rather drowned than discard their clothing.

The second ridiculous rule was that we were not allowed to play zithers. Pam and I laughed at that one. Who owned a zither anyway? I certainly didn't, and I had never seen one in the music department, but it was odd having that in the rule books.

A zither is a stringed instrument, like a guitar or lute, but it can have a lot more strings. It's an ancient instrument, its origins are Japan and China, and the ones that became popular in the US were from Europe.

I pretty much forgot about the boat and the zither for the next few years. I wasn't getting in a boat and I didn't have a zither.

One Saturday afternoon, when I wanted to relax or read, Ann and I were asked to clean out the attic.

I didn't even know the old place had an attic. The convent, with bedrooms for thirty of us, was old. It was probably built in the late 1800's, like the church across the street.

I had never even thought about the many nuns who had probably lived there all those years. I really didn't care about any of them, especially at this point.

Ann and I grudgingly walked up the narrow back steps to

the attic and opened the small wooden door. The attic was dusty, with books everywhere. Mostly old textbooks, but furniture, bed springs, bedposts, old typewriters, and rolled-up carpets were thrown all over the huge attic. I had no idea what we were supposed to do with any of the stuff. Were we supposed to dust it or get rid of it?

We drew straws, and Ann went back downstairs to ask Janine exactly what she meant by "clean the attic." Turns out even she wasn't sure, so we ended up moving a lot of books and furniture to one end where they could be taken downstairs by the maintenance man and thrown out.

I was looking through some stacks of chemistry textbooks, apparently written before the periodic table was discovered, when I saw an old package wrapped in brown paper wrapping.

There were holes in the paper, probably from mice or rats. I picked it up carefully, but the paper fell to dust in my hands. Underneath the wrapping was a zither.

I started laughing. Ann, with a wet rag in one hand and her long black hair pulled back into a ponytail, asked, "What's so funny?"

"It's a zither."

"A what?"

"It's a musical instrument, like a guitar."

"And why is that funny?"

"Because it's an old rule in the rule book. We weren't supposed to play them."

"What?"

"No really. It's one of those stupid rules that's never been changed."

"Here, let me try to play it."

She plucked a few dusty, horribly out-of-tune strings. Most of them had broken.

Ann handed it back to me.

"It sounds terrible. Maybe that's why it's forbidden."

"Well," I took it back from her. "Maybe it's because it's old, broken and out-of-tune. And you have no idea how to play it."

"Well, it could be that too," she acknowledged with a shrug.

224

I held the zither in my hands and wondered about its story.

Was it taken from some daring young nun who had sneaked it into the convent? Was it from someone who tried to learn how to play it and given up, to be relegated to the attic?

There were hundreds of thousands of pianos like that, once hopeful, but now just old useless pieces of furniture that no one played.

I should have kept the zither. Part of me wanted to, the last rule that I would ever break, but I set it down with the trash to be taken away. It was beyond repair.

It was only a few years ago, while I was looking up a picture of the old convent in Washington on the Internet, that I discovered the second reason Washington was famous. It wasn't just the corn-cob pipe factory, although that would have been enough of a claim to fame.

A zither factory in Washington manufactured over 11,000 zithers between 1860 and 1952. It had been the zither capital of the United States.

I suppose it was better than being the murder capital of the US, which St. Louis held for quite a few years and probably still does.

As a church musician, I do know now why there was such a rule. The Catholic church was very picky about its music. The organ reigned supreme, along with the Latin Mass, and the ageless Gregorian chant.

Guitars, lutes, zithers, and all those "sinful secular" instruments were banned from the Catholic liturgy for centuries.

When the church reformed itself at the Second Vatican Council in the 60's, Latin was thrown out, and Gregorian chant was pitched in the trash. The reform left everyone scrambling for music to play during the services. A good eleven centuries of music was no longer usable, with nothing to take its place. A whole era of hastily written, badly performed music was in store for the church.

Musicians were caught in the fight between the conservatives who wanted to go back to the old ways, and the liberals who thought the reforms were worth it.

For many years, the battle raged. Latin was back in, no, out. Some Gregorian chant was ok. Guitars were in--now out. People chose their masses depending on whether it was the organ or the guitar mass. Confusion was everywhere. Guitars and pianos were the rage--until they weren't. We scrambled to find the right balance. No one ever found it.

Once at my job as music director at church, I had the choir sing a 12th century Alleluia with a simple guitar accompaniment. An old lady came up to me as I tried to sneak out after mass. She was irate. "Why don't you ever play any of the old music?" she asked angrily. I didn't even know how to answer her. It would have taken too much time to explain.

I wonder how much trouble "Sister Mary" got into, when she innocently brought a zither into the convent, and how quickly it got confiscated and sent up to the attic?

Chapter 65
The Barnyard

February is a depressing month in the Midwest. Christmas is over--not much to look forward to. Cold and sleet, a little snow, grey skies, trudging to school every morning, even though it was only half a block away. The classes were tedious. Even my creative writing class became tiresome. Spring was a long way off. I still walked down to the river a few times a week, but it was cold. We had tryouts for the senior musical, "My Fair Lady," and so I was even busier than ever.

One evening I had a terrible sore throat, and I told S. Janine that I didn't know if I'd be able to teach the next morning. Sure enough, I woke up with a fever, and my throat felt like I was swallowing shards of glass.

Janine told me that S. Inez would be teaching a few of my English classes, and S. Christeta would be the sub for my creative writing class. I gave S. Janine my lesson plans, drank some hot tea, swallowed some Tylenol, and tried to sleep the day away.

S. Christeta was old and retired, probably in her late 70's or 80's. I was young, so I didn't know how old she was. She was tiny and had a hunched back. I don't even remember what she taught. I think she had one home economics class, but mostly was retired. I didn't like her. No, it wasn't that I didn't like her. I had barely spoken a word to her in one and a half years. She had a sour, tight look on her face. She seemed to be unhappy with everything, or at least that's what she looked like. She represented the "old nun," disapproving, conservative, judgmental, the kind of Christian that I hoped I would never become.

Janine knocked on my door later in the afternoon, after school was over. She looked upset. I wasn't feeling any better. Pat had brought me hot tea after school, and I drank some of the lukewarm liquid.

Janine stared at me. "Your class was horrible to Sister Christeta."

I nodded and wondered what she meant. I couldn't say anything without hurting.

"She was teaching them, and one of the boys started

making pig-like sounds, and then all of them made horrible barnyard sounds like cows and pigs and geese and sheep, and poor Sister Christeta ran out of the room in tears. She came down to my office, and I took over the rest of the class. They behaved after I yelled at them. But they are a terrible, undisciplined class. You need to keep better control over them!"

She looked at me disapprovingly, like I had personally recruited each animal sound and then picked the best ones, waiting for that day when a substitute took over.

"I'm really sorry that happened," was all I could say. Even that hurt.

In my four months of teaching them, I had never had any discipline problems. Oh, they had all laughed when I told them they could get A's, especially Wayne, but it was all good-hearted, honest reactions. They weren't easy, but I never had a moment where I wanted to cry or run out of the classroom. In fact, I enjoyed teaching them.

I could see them acting that way with Christeta, though, especially if she got that tight-lipped, sneering look of disapproval, and treated them like they were worthless.

After Janine left the room, I realized what I would have to do. I had to apologize to Christeta, even though it wasn't my fault, and I had to talk to the class about what they had done.

And I did both those things. But I always wondered what it had sounded like, those barnyard sounds from fifteen loud and raucous boys, most of whom lived on farms and could actually do authentic impressions.

The class doubled down and did extra well for a month or so, producing some of their best writing.

Poor Sister Christeta, who had never said more than two words to me anyway, said even fewer after that, and avoided making eye contact with me for the rest of the year. I think she was afraid that I would start mooing and oinking just like my students.

I could see her knowing glance in the morning when I was late for prayer. Yes, I'm sure she knew far earlier than I that I was going to leave. She had seen it happen too many times, the carefree casual attitude toward prayer and duties. She didn't allow herself the slightest imperfection. Kind when kindness was called for,

228

severe when the situation demanded it, clean, punctual, devoted to Christ. I don't recall ever seeing her smile. I'm sure she knew that I couldn't make it in religious life. I wonder if she knew that when I thought of her, I was glad I was going to leave.

Chapter 66
The Organ

I love the piano. I'm an excellent pianist, and I've played since I was five years old. I've played concerts, given lessons for many years, and practiced every day. It's a wonderful part of my life.

But I've always hated the organ. I'm not sure why, except it always represented "old" to me. The kind of church music and attitude that we wanted to get rid of. It was and is an irrational hatred. The instrument itself is amazing, and capable of so many different sounds--almost like a synthesizer for its time.

Bach wrote for the organ, and I love Bach. But I just know if he had owned a piano, he would have written everything for the piano instead of the organ. I tell myself that.

In the convent, I had to learn how to play the organ. I was a nun and a musician, so the chances were that wherever I went, I would be playing at a church. Lucky me.

I hated every moment of it. My hands were playing at a university level, and my feet, big feet, were playing the foot pedals at a pre-kindergarten level. I suffered through every organ lesson in college, along with S. Alexis, my organ teacher, who undoubtedly suffered even more.

Luckily, when I went to Washington on mission, I wasn't the main organist for the church. Thank God.

But every so often, I had to play an early weekday Mass. I think it was at 6 am, although I've easily blocked that memory from my mind.

The parish had been started in 1833. I don't know when the church was built, but by the time I got there in 1970, it was very old. What I hated the most, besides actually playing the organ, was that the choir loft sloped slightly downward to where the organ was, at the edge of the choir loft, like the organ was too heavy for the floor.

I hated balancing on the organ bench, leaving my feet free to pedal. With the piano, my feet were solidly on the floor, but I always felt shaky and unbalanced on the organ bench. And the feeling that the floor was sloping, and in danger of collapsing, was just too much.

One morning I woke up, remembered that I had to play the early morning service, and rushed over to the church after some useless black coffee.

It was cold outside, with a fresh sprinkling of snow covering the ground, and it was freezing in the church. I fumbled with the key to the loft, rubbed my hands together to warm them, changed into my organ shoes, turned on the beast, and it was time to start the first hymn.

I don't remember the name of the hymn, but the notes practically blasted out all five people in the front pews. And it certainly woke me up, much more effectively than the coffee. The stops were all pulled out, not pushed in. The last organist must have played a very loud postlude on Sunday, and never bothered to cancel the settings.

When I glanced down below, all five parishioners had turned around and were staring at me. The priest had a sour look on his face. I had to make a split-second decision. If I stopped, I'd have to reset everything quickly, and I knew I didn't have the ability to do that. I wasn't that good. Everyone was awake and paying attention at that point, so I just kept going. They wouldn't go to sleep--yet. I couldn't hear anything except the overpowering sound of the organ. I doubt if anyone was singing. I think the old wooden rafters were actually shaking. The floor certainly was. I wasn't sure how much more it could take before it collapsed.

The hymn had many verses, but that morning it had only one. I played it about twice as fast as it should have been, since no one was singing, at least I couldn't hear them, and I really wanted to get to the end of the hymn. I reset the organ and the rest of the Mass went smoothly. Afterwards I went down the steps and out the side door in record time.

I was thankful for a regular teaching day. No one ever mentioned the organ faux-pas, but every time I played any organ after that, I was very careful to check the stops and the volume pedal before I started.

Nothing in my life ever changed my attitude toward the "king" of instruments. I tried to realize its grandeur and greatness as one of the first musical instruments. The variety of sounds were incredible. The piano had only one sound. It didn't help. I was music director in a large Catholic parish for six years, and I managed to procure a synthesizer for the choir loft, but I still had to play the organ all too often.

A lot of people assumed I loved the organ. I was Catholic, a musician. I loved Bach--I was a music director at a Catholic church. What was there not to love? Plenty!

Chapter 67
Learning to Type

Besides acquiring some much-needed vices, I figured I better have some practical skills in case I had to work in business when I left. In high school I was too snobbish to take a typing class. My sisters were both secretaries, and I wanted so much more than that. Typing was what you took if you couldn't handle the real classes, the classes that would get you into a good college. My high school helped promote that attitude. Typing was on the same level as home economics and sewing--it wasn't a fancy college prep class. I never learned to type. I could peck at letters and got by doing that.

After four years in college and a year teaching, I realized that typing is a good skill to know. For someone who loved to write, and who was a teacher, it was unfortunate that my stupid prejudices got in the way.

I asked Sister Linda, the typing teacher, to help me learn. She gave me the big maroon book that began with, "The fox jumped over the hen or the fence," or something like that.

I practiced a little every night in the large typing room with its rows of typewriters on long tables, almost identical to the classroom at school. There was always someone in there, typing up lesson plans. It's amazing how motivation helps in learning something. I knew as a teacher or a secretary or whatever I would be, I wouldn't be typing numbers, so I skipped over those. I did fine with the letters and after about four months, practicing a little every night, I was very proficient at my new-found skill--and proud of it.

When I finally left that summer, I moved back to my parent's house and tried to find a job. I applied to become a Kelly girl--temporary clerical help. They hired me! I was called and asked to report to a lumber company the next Monday for work. I arrived in Florissant, a suburb of St. Louis, bright and early the next morning. I tried to look professional in my one and only blue dress. I would need to get a few more clothes quickly. They were pleased to have me and said they would need me for the entire week. The regular secretary handed me what looked like a ream of papers and I sat down at the typewriter. This was good. I had practiced and knew my stuff.

I looked at the first page. There were five columns of numbers. The kind of wood in a coded number, the price, the number of pieces in stock, and the order number for new wood. All numbers, rows and rows of them, pages and pages. I picked my way through the day, and although I was a hard worker, I probably didn't get a whole lot done. It was a very long week. My mom went with me to buy some clothes, which was fun, but it didn't make up for my misery at work. I really learned my numbers, though, even though they didn't ask me to come back the following week. I wasn't sure if it was because I finished most of the inventory, or I was really bad. I didn't ask.

Chapter 68

May 1972

The summer light woke me, streaming in between the slats of the blinds. It was Saturday. School had just let out for summer vacation, and I was leaving the convent. My parents were waiting anxiously for my call when I got to St. Louis.

I woke up at six that morning, skipped Mass and prayers as usual. I had skipped a lot of prayers in the last six months. What was the point?

I could hear Mass being said in the chapel right below my bedroom. The muted sounds of the nuns replying, then the acapella melody of "All Creatures of our God and King" reached up the stairs. I was glad I was alone. I stood in my little room, with my red and orange rug curled up in the corner, ready to go with me. My trunk was in the corner with my habits, three blue skirts and three white blouses. I wouldn't need them again. I carefully slipped on my only real dress--the same blue silk I wore that day I entered six years before. It slipped on easily since I had lost weight. I felt almost naked in the light silk.

My hair had been growing for months, and as I brushed it I heard a knock at the door. It was Sister Janine. We walked silently down the staircase and met the janitor in the front hall. He got my other suitcase filled with music and books. I went back in my room for a final look. It was bare now. The twin bed and cheap bookshelves were ready for the next sister who would arrive in a few months. The view out the window was nice, but there was nothing of me left in the room. Just four walls and a bed and desk that I used. I felt nothing as I turned and walked back downstairs to where Patricia and Inez were now waiting. Pat had a meeting at the motherhouse, and Inez had a dentist appointment somewhere in South St. Louis. They were going into the city anyway, so that was why they had volunteered to take me.

We stood in the front hall for a few minutes and I hoped someone else would come to say goodbye. But no one did. My self-confidence fell even lower.

I thought I wouldn't care, but I did. The least they could

have done was to say goodbye. There were thirty-one nuns in the convent and it was a Saturday morning. It wasn't like they had so many important things to do now that school was over. I waited a few more minutes, took a last look down the corridor and into the old parlor, with its overstuffed chairs, and walked out the front door.

I reached up to push my veil back, but just felt my hair. I was free. Inez drove and Pat sat in the front seat with her. I got the back seat. I knew Pat would miss me a little, but Inez was harder to read. She was too busy with her teaching and the theatre department to ever talk to me at all. She was always kind, but aloof.

I watched the hot asphalt of Highway 100 under the car as the green fields blurred by, the telephone wires swirling and dipping as we drove. Inez and Pat talked about Kevin and Joan, two seniors who had showed so much promise academically, won scholarships to college, and then got pregnant and married, those dreams gone quickly. I didn't know them and I realized I didn't care. My ears tuned them out as I watched us turn onto Highway 44 leading into St. Louis. All I could think about was my new life ahead of me.

We passed by the large power plant close to the city.

My parents were picking me up at the motherhouse. I would call them from the office, and then wait the twenty minutes for them to drive down from north St. Louis.

We turned right on Ripa Avenue. We passed a few poor homes, the high school, and then the motherhouse loomed in front of us. Pat helped me with the heaviest suitcase and together we lugged them up to the door. I turned to say goodbye to Inez.

She gave me a quick hug and said, "Good luck with everything." And that was it.

Pat and I put my suitcases in a parlor by the front door, and I walked with Pat down to the main office, where I asked if I could use the phone. I didn't know the sister who pushed the phone towards me.

"Hi, Mom. I'm here. Just pick me up by the front entrance. I'll be looking for you."

The sister working at the desk didn't look at me as she took

236

the receiver and put it back on the phone.

Pat said, "My meeting is over in the other building. I'll say my goodbyes here. You ok?"

"I'm fine, you go ahead--and thanks for bringing me."

She turned to go, and then turned back.

"Hey, good luck with everything. Let me know how you're doing."

We walked into the corridor and she went in the opposite direction. I watched her, wondering if I would ever see her again.

Hoping I wouldn't run into anyone I knew, I walked past the chapel, feeling almost guilty in my pale blue dress with no veil.

Guilty of what? Leaving? Not dressing correctly? I wasn't sure. Maybe it was just years of guilt piled up in layers.

Two older sisters walked by me and stared, wondering what I was doing there.

I pushed open the swinging doors and headed back toward the postulant wing.

A group of postulants walked by. One of them whispered something to another one. I didn't know them. They looked awfully young.

The parlor was welcoming with my suitcases and rug and I sat down on a wingback chair. I looked at the driveway and front lawn, where my classmates and I walked every morning and evening for four years. It seemed such a long time ago, but it had only been two years since I had left the motherhouse.

The trees were completely leafed out, their green covering any glimpse of the Mississippi River.

I hoped no one would walk by. I didn't feel like talking to anyone at the motherhouse. I got up and closed the door almost all the way so that no one could see in.

I glanced around the parlor, with its decorative molding halfway up the walls, and the pale green wallpaper above, peeling around the door. The rug had a worn brown and green floral pattern, threadbare in front of the four upholstered chairs. I felt the weight of the building all around and over me. What used to be fun and exciting, exploring the hundreds of rooms, sneaking out on the roof that first Christmas, being terrified in the basement catacombs, was in reality just a sameness repeated endlessly, like so many prayers that had come to nothing. Everything seemed old and drab this morning.

The motherhouse was not living or breathing. Yet as I sat alone in the silent parlor, I felt its judgment and guilt pressing down on me, wrapping me in swaths of wool fabric and the old tight veil. I didn't want to think about the hundred years of history, from the concrete foundations up to the bell tower, the endless prayers, the nuns who had lived here, slept here, died here.

I didn't want to think about the four years I had wasted here. Had I wasted them? I got an education, a degree, a credential, made friends, but I had done more than that. I had grown up, not because of all the instructions and rules, but in between all of them, in spite of them. I had learned what was important in my life: God, friendship, freedom. Those were important.

I thought about my "leave of absence." Who was I kidding? I had decided in some remote corner of my mind that I could always come back if things didn't work out, but as I sat there, I knew without a doubt that I would never come back. My back-up plan was torn up in my mind, the pages shredded and thrown in the trash.

I could already greedily breathe in the freedom. It was a hot and sticky freedom in the May air, but I was truly free, suddenly and unexpectedly.

I knew it wouldn't be easy. I was free to find a job, make a living, make mistakes, find out what life was about outside the convent walls. Some of it would be hard work, and lonely, but this was my new beginning. I was twenty-four years old, and ready to do great things with my life. I just wasn't sure what they would be.

As I watched the heat rising from the asphalt, my parents' old white Valiant pulled around the corner and tentatively stopped by the front entrance. They weren't exactly sure where to park.

My dad opened the car door and got out, smiling as always.

I jumped up, grabbed both suitcases, pulling one behind me, and tucked the rug under my arm. I took a final glance at the dim room, the musty carpets, the long corridor that I had cleaned and polished stretching into the dim light.

The motherhouse, solid and unforgiving, barely glanced at me as I struggled down the corridor to the door. I turned around once, then pushed open the large carved wooden door. It no longer had any power over me.

My mom and dad, smiling widely, walked up the stairs and gave me a hug. Dad took a suitcase and I handed Mom the rug. The door slowly closed on the darkness inside as I stepped out into the bright summer light. I didn't look back.

Epilogue

My first job after leaving the convent was the ill-fated typing job where I had to type numbers instead of letters. But I was able to find a second job as a waitress at the St. Louis airport. I started at 5:30 every morning. I was used to getting up early and enjoyed having the rest of the afternoon and evening free. My dad counted all my tips every afternoon, glad for something to do, since he had just retired. My parents were thrilled to have me home, but sad that I would be leaving for California soon, another one of those decisions that they couldn't understand. I knew it was just for a little while, to establish my independence and my ability to make my way in the world. It was something I felt I had to do, and I could do it with a friend and a teaching job almost made to order.

Patrice flew in from California in August, and we packed up my meager belongings in the trunk of my new Duster, generously given to me by my parents, and set off for my new life. I was sure I would return to St. Louis in a few years, but this was an adventure I couldn't pass up, and I didn't want to be like so many ex-nuns I knew who only had other nuns as their friends. An ex-nun was better than a nun.

My new job was to teach music and religion at San Gabriel Catholic High School in San Gabriel, California. It was part of the old San Gabriel Mission complex. Father Serra had built a string of missions up the California coast in the 1700's as he was converting the Indians to Christianity, and most of the missions were still standing, even though many had suffered through earthquakes and age.

I somehow made it through two years of teaching, never really understanding or trying to understand my Hispanic students or their background. I was too busy trying to get my life on track. I didn't know where the track was, or where it would be going, but I regarded teaching as a necessary duty to make enough money to survive.

After a few months my roommate Patrice became very upset when I agreed to go on a date with a young black professor at UCLA. It wasn't a racial thing. She said, "But what am I going to do on a Friday night!"

We had done everything together those first few months, and enjoyed each other's company, but I was not interested in another "particular friendship" and told her I wanted to date and someday get married. The whole confusion about friendships followed me out to California and led to some very difficult and awkward moments. We didn't speak much after that. That was the end of our friendship. My thrill of being able to pick my roommate turned to despair that I had made the wrong choice yet again.

After a few short months, my first boyfriend didn't work out, but my second one did. His name was Don and he turned out to be pretty special. He was an engineer, smart, kind, honest, and he loved me. It took many proposals before I said yes to him. It wasn't that I didn't love him. I had only been out of the convent eight months when I met him and had only dated one other person. I wasn't ready for marriage. But he was thankfully persistent, and I finally agreed to marry him. We will be celebrating our 46th anniversary this year.

We have two wonderful children, a son named David and a daughter Laura, and a lifetime of amazing memories with them and their spouses Heather and Carlos. We almost lost our daughter when she was attacked by a mountain lion at age five, and that story became the basis for my first book, "Out of the Lion's Den."

I never moved back to St. Louis and we stayed in the Orange County area all our lives. Don worked in the optical industry and the jobs were on the West Coast. I taught piano and became music director at a large Catholic church. But Laura's attack made me rethink everything I had ever believed in, and I gave up the Catholic church, all its beliefs and became an atheist.

I realized that the God who had meant so much to me and formed my life and choices didn't even exist. I am very happy with my atheism and feel that even though it brings less comfort than religion, it is as close to the truth as I will ever get. And I'd rather have truth. I am a secular humanist. I do have values and beliefs: honesty, justice, kindness, compassion, truth. It's simply that I don't believe in any supernatural beings. I am constantly amazed at the people I've met who share that same worldview and have met quite a circle of friends who are wonderful and caring.

I was in touch with Pam for years, then lost track of her as we both moved. But one summer I found her again and we reconnected. We are now the best friends we never were when we were younger, and I'm very grateful she's such an important part of my life. And I'm still friends with Louise, the violinist, who left the order and moved back to Oregon.

A group contacted me a few years ago on Facebook by the name of "Convent Chicks", a small group of sisters and ex-sisters from my class. Juliette was part of the group and a few others mentioned in the book. It's strange to hear bits and pieces about them now since I lost track of them at age twenty-two. I wouldn't recognize or know any of them, but it was and is fun to catch up with their lives.

Another time, when I was in St. Louis, I met up with Pam, and on a stormy afternoon with a tornado warning blaring from the city sirens, we and my daughter and daughter-in-law drove down to the motherhouse.

The nun who answered the door said, "I know you! You're Lady Bach! Get in here. There's a tornado warning!" I couldn't believe this nun, who'd been a few classes behind me, remembered me after all those years, and even remembered a nickname I barely recalled myself.

We stood lined up with the other nuns in the basement hall. For some reason I wasn't the least bit worried. I knew how thick those walls were! After the storm passed, although a tornado did hit just a few miles away, we walked the halls with a nun from our old class, chatting with people we remembered. A lot of people remembered Pam, and I was happy to see many of my old classmates and even a few teachers!

The huge motherhouse was now mostly empty, but small groups of sisters still lived and worked in parts of it. I met Elena, who was still there working. She had been out on the roof with me that first Christmas. Sadly, she didn't remember the moment at all.

We talked with other sisters and showed Laura and Heather the new elevators, thank God, and the large staircase that rose up to the fourth floor. The grandfather clock still stood watching the corridors I had cleaned. The chapel had been completely modernized, with new tile floors, chairs instead of old wooden pews, but the stained- glass windows were still there.

Not once, especially that day at the motherhouse reminiscing, did I regret my decision to leave. Going back dredged up so many memories, both good and bad, that I hardly knew which ones to remember: the bell tower, S. Regina, the old elevators, the catacombs of the basement, the size of the motherhouse, the long corridors, the emptiness of the once bustling city. I was thrilled to show my family the places I had talked about for years. I felt overwhelmed at the tension in my whole body and the feeling of power that the motherhouse still held after all those years.

Even though I entertained my family with my convent stories and hope you have enjoyed many of them in this book, the basic problems of women in religious life has never really been resolved.

First of all, I don't claim to be an expert on religious life. Even though everything in my book actually occurred, I am only able to write about my own experience. Other sisters had lives much different than mine, I'm sure. I have not been a part of religious life for many years and have deliberately distanced myself from its trials and difficulties. But I am very aware that the promises and the possibilities of the early sixties and seventies never came to fruition. All anyone has to do is look at the statistics. The number of sisters has fallen from 180,000 in 1965 to about 31,000 in 2019. And only 1% of those nuns are below the age of 40. These are ominous numbers for the future of sisters in this country.

Could the church have changed these numbers? I don't know if they could have increased the number of vocations, but they certainly could have stopped the massive exodus of sisters. They could have given women more equality with men, more power to control and run institutions and make rules and regulations for themselves instead of being controlled by men.

Even now in 2021, Pope Francis rejects the idea of women becoming priests or even having more control over their own destinies. I didn't know any nuns that wanted to become priests, but I knew many women who wanted to be equal to men in their ability to make decisions for themselves and their orders. They were never given the chance.

As soon as I walked out those doors, I experienced freedom and I was and always will be grateful for it. I no longer lived my life bound by arbitrary rules made centuries ago that served no discernible purpose. I no longer had to wait to see the validity of some ridiculous rule that made no sense. I no longer had to fight hard for something I could achieve simply by walking out the door.

The church blamed a lot of the problems on secularism, the loss of prayer in the schools and the lack of religion. But the church was to blame for its rigid adherence to the past, its refusal to respect the equality between men and women, and its unquestioning acceptance to meaningless traditions of the past. I think that if the church had been able to continue its modernization, the number of nuns and clergy wouldn't have dropped so drastically.

School Sisters of Notre Dame

Dedication

The first dedication is to my family. My husband Don, son David and his wife Heather listened to all these stories over the years with great patience. And I am especially grateful to my daughter Laura, without whom I would probably never have told the stories in the first place. When she was recovering in the hospital after her mountain lion attack at age five, I told her I would be back to visit her soon, but she was confused about reading the clock on the wall. That's when I first told her the story of Juliette and the bell, and how Juliette got confused about reading the little hand and the big hand of the clock. It was a great way of teaching her how to tell time. Laura was in the hospital for over forty days so there was plenty of opportunity to tell her stories. She loved hearing about Pam and Juliette, the basement of the motherhouse and the bell tower. It was because of her that I began to think that someday I might write a book about my many experiences those six years.

Even though I left the order, I would like to also dedicate the book to the sisters who remained in the order and dedicated their lives to teaching. There were many conservative and difficult sisters who made my life miserable, but there were just as many who tried to modernize the order and make it relevant for this century and beyond. It's unfortunate that they were not appreciated as they should have been. S. Rachel is still a member of the order, even though I lost track of her years ago. After I left, a very progressive sister was put in charge of the order but I have no idea how her reforms affected it. The only people I kept up with were friends who left the order, not the ones who stayed. I do know that the plight of sisters today in 2020 is probably irredeemable, judging from the depleted numbers of sisters in this country and their advanced ages.

But for all my disappointment in the order, I do respect those who stayed and made the best of it, took their vows seriously, and tried to do their jobs as well as they could. I have a lot of admiration for them and appreciate all that they have contributed to the education of so many students across the country.

I would like to thank my editor, Marcia Sargent. Without her help, patience and encouragement, I would have never published this book. I would also like to thank my daughter Laura for the cover art and Ramon Swain for the design. Thanks to all who helped me bring this book to publication.

Author's Biography

 Susan K. Mattern is the author of "Out of the Lion's Den," the story of her daughter's mountain lion attack, her recovery, and the lawsuit and trial against the County of Orange in California. Raised a Catholic, she joined a convent for six years but became an atheist after her daughter was almost killed. An accomplished pianist, she loves Bach, is happily married and is grateful for her two loving children and their spouses.

 You can contact her on her websites, http://susanmattern.com or http://outofthelionsden.net, or on Instagram https://www.instagram.com/mattern.susan/

Made in the USA
Monee, IL
21 June 2022

98405579R00138